Meeting the global crisis

Kingdom community, diaconal church and a diaconal world

— DAVID CLARK —

Sacristy Press

Sacristy Press
PO Box 612, Durham, DH1 9HT

www.sacristy.co.uk

First published in 2023 by Sacristy Press, Durham

Copyright © David Clark 2023
The moral rights of the author have been asserted.

All rights reserved, no part of this publication may be reproduced or transmitted in any form or by any means, electronic, mechanical photocopying, documentary, film or in any other format without prior written permission of the publisher.

Scripture quotations, unless otherwise stated, are from the New Revised Standard Version Bible: Anglicized Edition, copyright © 1989, 1995 National Council of the Churches of Christ in the United States of America. Used by permission. All rights reserved worldwide.

Every reasonable effort has been made to trace the copyright holders of material reproduced in this book, but if any have been inadvertently overlooked the publisher would be glad to hear from them.

Sacristy Limited, registered in England & Wales, number 7565667

British Library Cataloguing-in-Publication Data
A catalogue record for the book is available from the British Library

ISBN 978-1-78959-303-7

Contents

Foreword iv
Introduction... 1
Summary... 4

Chapter 1. The communal imperative............................ 8
Chapter 2. What is community? 12
Chapter 3. A Christian symbolic universe..................... 18
Chapter 4. The kingdom community............................. 24
Chapter 5. Building the kingdom community 45
Chapter 6. A Christian symbolic universe for the twenty-first
    century 64
Chapter 7. The process of communal institutionalization today..... 92
Chapter 8. Kingdom community building in practice.............. 99
Chapter 9. A new paradigm—the diaconal church 137
Chapter 10. Creating a diaconal world: Diaconal institutions...... 180

Appendix 1. Biblical references for attributes of the gifts of the
    kingdom community..................................... 193
Appendix 2. Twelve signs of the human city 198
Appendix 3. Twenty theses for 202
Appendix 4. The deacon in action—a personal perspective........ 208

Bibliography 218

Foreword

*"The urgent task before humankind is the
creation of a diaconal (servant) world"*
David Clark

It's time for the global church to work together to further God's kingdom here on earth. We can no longer stay in our silos, but need to work together for peace, justice and to enable all of God's children to flourish. More than ever, we are called to servant leadership.

As a rostered Deacon in the Evangelical Lutheran Church in America, (ELCA) as well as a member of the ELCA Deaconess Community, it is exciting to have the work of David Clark published on the this often mis-understood concept of Diakonia.

After having had the honor of working with David as he finished up his research, it was evident that he has a heart for the diaconate, especially as it pertains to working together in community. Church membership has and continues to decline. The world is changing and it is time that the focus of the church needs to be one that focuses on the building up of the community, both inside and outside the walls of the church. The church has not only the opportunity but is being called to focus on the many global crises of our time. Now more than ever, the church and its members are called to "prophetic diakonia".

Clark has studied the work of The Revd Dr Martin Luther King Jr and his concept of the "beloved community" which works to bring about God's kingdom here on earth. This understanding can dictate how the church functions in society. Servant leadership is at the forefront of this model and the use of deacons equipping the people to do this servant work is crucial.

I believe in order for the church to be an effective witness and change maker in this world, Clark's work is crucial for understanding how to change the institutional church to a church that reaches out across physical and spiritual borders to not only address the social problems we all face in this global community, but to help bring about God's kingdom here and now.

Sister Dr Dottie Almoney, ELCA Deacon
Director of Outreach and Education
St Peter's Lutheran Church, Lancaster, PA

Introduction

This book is a response from a Christian perspective to the crises of our era. The early decades of the twenty-first century have witnessed our world possessing the greatest potential for the wellbeing of humankind. Yet they have also produced the greatest threats to our survival in human history. The most urgent challenge is how we can best respond to the devastating consequences of climate change as the Secretary General of the United Nations made starkly clear in November 2022 at the commencement of the COP27 climate change conference in Egypt. However, other critical threats to the future of human civilization include the accumulation of weapons of mass destruction, new pandemics, the universality of "fake news" and the rise of authoritarian regimes.

Nevertheless, I have long believed that the crises we face, though daunting, are "presenting problems". Ultimately, the most fundamental challenge we face is how our world can become a global community of diverse communities. Unless this is achieved, no other crisis will be resolved. This means that "the quest for community", as Robert Nisbet called it soon after the Second World War, becomes the paramount task for this and all future generations.[1]

My own interest in the meaning and nature of community goes back to the 1960s when I spent five years as a Methodist minister in Woodhouse, a rural suburb of Sheffield, then being developed to house those moving from the inner-city areas of Brightside and Attercliffe. This situation was one issue addressed in my doctoral thesis concerning how such changes were affecting the life of Woodhouse as a community. Since then, I have explored the meaning of community, as a concept and in practice, in relation to the future of the church, education, the workplace and the life

---

[1] R. A. Nisbet, *The Quest for Community* (Wilmington, DE: ISI Books, 2010 [1953]).

of the city. I have sought to combat the trivializing of the concept through overuse and to demonstrate the tremendous power of community, for good or ill, in a diversity of social contexts.

However, it is what Christian faith, through the life of the church *and* beyond, has to offer to our understanding and practice of community that has been my particular concern. I continue to believe that the Christian faith has a unique contribution to make to addressing the crises of our time, a contribution which I spell out in this book. Nevertheless, I am convinced that, for this vision to become a reality, there will need to be profound changes in the life and leadership of the church both locally and worldwide. Neither the model of Christendom nor that of the Reformation can any longer suffice. I am also convinced that what is the immediate need is a communal theology of mission which offers meaning and hope to individuals, human collectives and our world alike.

This quest for community requires a theology of mission which reinstates the centrality of the kingdom, that which, in the context of today's world, I call "the kingdom community". Such a theology takes the Trinity as its "model", diversity in unity and unity embracing diversity, and representing community at its zenith. The Trinity is sovereign over a kingdom community which embodies the Trinitarian gifts of life, liberation, love, learning and servant leadership. The nature and meaning of the kingdom community and its gifts are informed and elucidated by the insights of both sociology and theology. I believe it is a kingdom-centred understanding of the nature of community which now needs to guide the communal quest of not only the church but every human collective. Until this happens humankind will be unable to tackle the immensely difficult task ahead of how to survive and flourish.

It is this understanding of community which must in future shape the mission and life of the church. The medium must be the message. This will mean the emergence of a diaconal or servant church with the people of God as its primary resource, and a leadership, including its diaconal leadership, refashioned to meet the communal needs of today. It will also mean a church committed to acquiring a deeper understanding and expression in practice of what it means, as the hymnwriter Edward Hayes Plumptre puts it, for there to be "one church, one faith, one Lord" (Ephesians 4:5–6).

Whilst writing this book, I have become increasingly aware of the affinity of many of the concepts I have been exploring with Catholic Social Teaching (CST).[2] There are some notable differences between my approach and that of CST. For example, I take a more experiential stance to a communal theology; CST is more deductive, with a greater reliance on the insights of natural law.[3] My concern is with a kingdom theology; CST rarely mentions the kingdom, it is the teaching of the church which remains centre-stage.

Nevertheless, CST mirrors as well as helps to fill out a number of my convictions as to how the mission of the church can become more relevant to the crises which our world currently faces. I mention some of those affinities in the body of my book. Akin to the intention of Anna Rowlands with regards to CST, my concern is to reinstate the concept of community "even when we cannot guarantee that it can produce the necessary social solutions we crave and even when it can be co-opted by dark forces".[4] My hope, like that of Rowlands for CST, is to offer a vision of society and world "conditioned not solely by the life of necessity … but rooted in an argument for the value of a transcendent account of freedom, beauty and goodness for the possibility of making all things new". As Rowlands observes, such contributions do not represent "a set of solutions to complex late modern problems, but they do articulate something of the ethical disposition required to keep open the horizons of struggle towards a better version of a common life".

---

[2] See here in particular: *Compendium of the Social Doctrine of the Roman Catholic Church* (English edition: London: Continuum, 2005); and Anna Rowlands, *Towards a Politics of Communion: Catholic Social Teaching in Dark Times* (London: T&T Clark, 2021).

[3] Rowlands, *Towards a Politics of Communion*, p. 33.

[4] Rowlands, *Towards a Politics of Communion*, p. 121.

Summary

1. The communal imperative
Human civilization today faces some of the most critical threats to its survival that it has experienced in its history. Nevertheless, the most fundamental challenge of all has been there all along. How can we learn to live together and flourish as a global community of diverse communities?

2. What is community?
Before this question can be explored, it is important to be clear what is meant by the term "community". From a sociological perspective, the strongest definition is community understood as "feeling", that is when people experience a sense of community—in particular a sense of security, of significance and of solidarity. These experiences are internalized as we grow through the process of socialization and social control.

The problem is that any purely affective definition reveals that community has a "dark side". This becomes clear when social collectives which possess a strong sense of community remain closed and hostile to other social collectives or seek to dominate them. This presents humankind with a "communal dilemma"—how can such closure be overcome and the way opened to the creation of a global community?

3. A Christian symbolic universe
To surmount the communal dilemma, it is necessary to embrace a worldview which can harness the positive power of community. Such a worldview is called by Berger and Luckmann "a symbolic universe".[5] The latter "integrates different provinces of meaning", including beliefs, values and norms, into a comprehensive worldview which gives meaning

---

[5] Peter Berger and Thomas Luckmann, *The Social Construction of Reality* (Harmondsworth: Penguin, 1966, 1984).

and purpose to the human collectives involved. Every symbolic universe is given "legitimation" by some widely acknowledged authority. The beliefs, values and norms which characterize a symbolic universe will determine for what societal ends, constructive or destructive, the power of community is exercised.

For two millennia, the West has been permeated by the beliefs and values of a Christian symbolic universe, although these have often been misinterpreted and distorted. Even though this universe has been challenged by other symbolic universes and is now less dominant, the historian Tom Holland believes that its legacy continues to shape Western culture.[6]

4. The kingdom community

This book argues that another term for this Christian symbolic universe is "the kingdom community". The problem of the word "kingdom" is discussed.

The sovereign of the kingdom community is the Trinity, exemplifying the meaning of community at its zenith. Through the kingdom community, the Trinity offers humankind five gifts—life, liberation, love, learning and servant leadership. These build on, transform and universalize the five primary sociological components of community already identified (a sense of security, significance and solidarity, socialization and social control). The power of these gifts is in particular channelled through Christian worship and historic Christian spiritualities.

Other models of the kingdom are reviewed, that with most affinity to the kingdom community being seen as "the beloved community", a vision for a universal and inclusive community espoused by Martin Luther King and his followers in their pursuit of civil rights in the USA.

It is argued that it is valid to speak of "building" the kingdom community.

---

[6] Tom Holland, *Dominion: The Making of the Western Mind* (London: Abacus, 2019).

5. Building the kingdom community

Berger and Luckmann believe that symbolic universes shape and control a society through a process of "institutionalization". This process is given impetus by symbolic figures, groups and social movements which, over time, introduce new beliefs and values, and the norms and customs deriving from them, into the life of established institutions. Following this process of societal transformation, a Christian symbolic universe reflecting the gifts of the kingdom community has shaped the history of the West. Nevertheless, the communal dilemma, the closure of strong communities, remains a major threat to the emergence of a global community of communities.

6. A Christian symbolic universe for the twenty-first century

Before looking at the practical process of communal institutionalization today, inspired by the vision of the kingdom community, the type of authority shaping a Christian symbolic universe is discussed. The nature of the five gifts of the kingdom community is also reviewed showing, through a number of significant texts, the depth of their meaning which needs to be explored as an ongoing journey of discovery. The universal and complementary importance of the five gifts is also stressed.

7. The process of communal institutionalization today

A Christian institutionalization process shaped by the gifts of the kingdom community continues today. This book illustrates that process with reference to a wide variety of symbolic figures, groups, social movements, organizations and communally emerging institutions, which manifest these gifts. Such social collectives can arise within and beyond established institutions, secular *or* sacred. The impact of this institutionalization process on today's quest for community is reviewed.

8. A new paradigm—the diaconal church

In the process of communal institutionalization, the church has a crucial and distinctive part to play. However, this can only be achieved if it breaks from Christendom *and* post-Reformation models of church, rediscovers and reaffirms its commission to be the servant of the kingdom community and becomes a "diaconal" church.

The diaconal church is both institution and movement. As institution, it is concerned with preserving, celebrating and building on the West's kingdom-centred legacy. As movement, it is committed to enabling every human collective, from the family to the nation, to manifest the gifts of the kingdom community. Its mission is undertaken primarily by the people of God in the world.

Within the diaconal church all forms of leadership are servant leadership. Presbyters form what is identified as "an order of continuity". They serve the church notably in its institutional form and predominantly as a community of place. They nurture and educate the people of God to understand, treasure and develop their kingdom-focused faith.

Within the diaconal church as movement, a renewed diaconate forms "an order of transformation". Its deacons have two main church-facing roles. As enablers and educators, they equip the people of God to be kingdom community builders in the world. Their main world-facing roles are those of catalyst, intermediary and partner. These involve them engaging with, affirming and resourcing those groups, movements and organizations working for the communal transformation of society and world.

Within the diaconal church, bishops form "an order of unity" drawing together the church as institution and movement and, to this end, co-ordinating the ministries of presbyters and deacons. A diaconal church is self-governing, committed to shared decision-making, to furthering subsidiarity and to encouraging partnerships. It takes ecumenism to be imperative.

9. Creating a diaconal world

The urgent task before humankind is the creation of a diaconal (servant) world. This will be a global community shaped and empowered by a Christian symbolic universe and the gifts of the kingdom community. Achieving such a world requires the creation of secular diaconal institutions. The form of these will in some important ways reflect that of the diaconal church; for example, their being shaped by the need for both continuity and movement. Servant leadership remains essential. The creation of such a world, a global community of communities, is an immense undertaking yet of critical importance if the crises now facing us are to be addressed and humankind is to survive and flourish.

1

The communal imperative

"The state we're in"—society and world

The world in the twenty-first century faces challenges of an unprecedented nature. As Pope Francis put it to the decennial national conference of the Italian church in 2015, "We are not living in an era of change but a change of era".

This change of era has brought challenges which, for the first time in human history, threaten the very survival of humankind. Paramount is global warming.[1] Its dire consequences, exacerbated by the exploitation of the earth's resources and the continuing pollution of the environment, point to many parts of the world where in the decades ahead it will be impossible for human beings to live. The flooding of a third of Pakistan in the summer of 2022 is but a foretaste of things to come. Yet the unwillingness at COP27 of many large nations to cut back on their use of fossil fuels bodes ill for the future.

One consequence of climate change will be mass economic migration, it being estimated that there could be 1.5 billion people on the move in the next 30 years.[2] That this could be managed, and even have some benefits, if nations were positively geared to receiving those on the move,

---

[1] Al Gore, *The Future* (London: W. H. Allen, 2013); Pope Francis, *Laudato Si': On care for our common home* (London: Catholic Truth Society, 2015). Most recently, the report of *The Intergovernmental Panel on Climate Change* (February 2022) <https://www.ipcc.ch/>, accessed 4 May 2023.

[2] P. Khanna, *Move: How Mass Migration will Reshape the World* (London: Weidenfeld & Nicolson, 2022).

is not in doubt. However, if such migration continues to be met with "walls" of resistance and hostility to "strangers", then the consequences will be a world tearing itself apart.

Humanity has only recently been reminded that it will be increasingly vulnerable to pandemics, now spread speedily and widely by international travel. This demands a concerted international response which was not in evidence during the Covid-19 pandemic. Then, there remain the human-made threats of sectarian conflict, terrorism and inter-state aggression. And, as the war in Ukraine has reminded us, there needs to be greater recognition that it may take only one leader with autocratic power to make the nightmare of a nuclear holocaust a reality.

This is not to ignore the fact that the advances of industry, science, technology and education have over recent centuries increased the wealth and wellbeing of millions. However, with these benefits have come the challenges of being able to handle wisely the potential dangers of discoveries such as nuclear energy, genetic advances and artificial intelligence. The arrival of the internet has offered a huge encyclopaedia of instant knowledge to billions across the globe and facilitated human connectivity in a way never before imagined. Nevertheless, it has also increased the influence of those prepared to exploit it and disfigure our humanity, individually and collectively. Alongside the impressive advances of humankind, therefore, much happening in our world today continues to reflect the shadow side of human nature. "The state we're in" offers immense promise yet remains acutely precarious with human survival itself in the balance.

The quest for community

My contention in this book is that though many of the crises humankind now faces are potentially terminal they are, in fact, "presenting problems". In short, they are crises which can only be overcome if we grasp that there is a more fundamental issue underpinning all of them. The reality is that the resolution of these crises ultimately depends on our resolving the challenge of *how humankind can live and work together as a global community of diverse communities*. Anna Rowlands, in considering Catholic Social Teaching, refers to Pope Francis who in *Fratelli tutti* argues that "what we have lost is a social commitment to the idea of fraternity—to seeing all people as a single human family, and the earth as our common home and a fully common and social ethic that embodies this".[3]

A critical choice lies ahead. We either allow our world to fragment with each nation seeking to preserve or expand its own territory and influence for its own benefit. This, I believe, would simply mean postponing disaster. Or we recognize that the creation of a world bound together by a concern for the good of all, whilst facilitating a rich diversity of cultures and lifestyles, is the only way in which humankind can survive and flourish.

For such a global community of communities to come into being, every human collective has to learn how to enhance its own strength as a community whilst being open to live and work together with others. Because such open relationships have been found so hard to achieve throughout history, I call this challenge "the communal dilemma". I describe the latter as "the problem which every social collective faces when the wellbeing of humankind requires that it becomes and remains open to others without undermining its own strength as a community".

There are many factors which persuade social collectives that closure is to be preferred to openness. I explore these more fully later when I reflect on "the dark side of community". Suffice it to say here that there is often fear of a loss of control when the values, norms and common practices which have sustained a human collective in the past appear to be threatened by other collectives. To take a very local example, in early 2022 Broughton Parish Council, near Preston in Lancashire, supported by a majority of residents, were up in arms opposing plans to build a "super mosque" on the outskirts of the village. On a much broader level, arguments for Brexit were founded on the claims that Britain had "lost control" of its own affairs and its identity was threatened by an overbearing Europe.

There are also human collectives which have sought to sustain or strengthen their communal life and heritage by force. In this case closure to the wider world is used to empower the aggressor and weaken the

---

[3] Anna Rowlands, *Towards a Politics of Communion: Catholic Social Teaching in Dark Times* (London: T&T Clark, 2021), p. 86.

victim. We witnessed this in the Second World War, saw it happening in Vietnam, the Balkans, Syria and Iraq, and now find it happening again in Ukraine.

The "state we're in" makes the luxury of keeping ourselves to ourselves impossible to justify. We now face "the quest for (a global) community" or extinction.[4] Such a quest can no longer remain a utopian dream; it is an imperative achievement if humankind is to survive. It is what Pope Francis calls "the struggle for communion".[5] Before the world became accessible to all, the quest for community could be confined to a particular neighbourhood, city or nation. Now, however, mobility—physical, cultural, social and mental—means that we are all increasingly aware that humankind is intimately interrelated and that we are living on a very small planet.[6] Until we recognize that none of us can survive unless all of us survive, the future for humankind looks bleak.

Even so, the quest for community is about much more than survival. It seeks a way in which human beings and the planet can flourish. In Christian terms, as I argue later, it is about a journey of discovery concerning how we can become whole individuals, families, neighbourhoods, institutions, cities and nations, and achieve "the integrity of creation".[7] In short, it is the search for communal wholeness, or "holiness",[8] and how to make that a reality.

Yet such a quest begs a crucial question. What do we mean by "community"? What is the nature of the journey and how shall we know when we have "arrived"? I believe that the discipline of sociology can help us to begin answering these fundamental questions.

---

[4] See Robert Nisbet, *The Quest for Community* (Wilmington, DE: ISI Books, 2010 [1953]).

[5] Rowlands, *Towards a Politics of Communion*, p. 300.

[6] See the facts relating to this set out in Khanna, *Move*, op. cit.

[7] Part of the commitment of the World Council of Churches during its Vancouver Assembly in 1983.

[8] This phrase has its origins in the Methodist concept of "social holiness". See David Clark (ed.), *Reshaping the Mission of Methodism: A Diaconal Church Approach* (Oldham: Church in the Marketplace Publications, 2010), pp. 172–80.

2

What is community?

A sociological perspective

"Community" is an ambiguous concept, not least because it is used unthinkingly in such a wide diversity of contexts.[1] The problem is that the very breadth of its use leads to the concept being trivialized. It has come to mean "all things to all people" and consequently little to anyone. One widely accepted understanding of the concept is that it means something "good", or at least "beneficent", a generalization I later question as simplistic and raising many problems.

As a sociologist, I have sought to tease out the meaning of "community" by focusing on *the context* in which the concept is used.[2] This shows that the clarity and strength of community increases the further we go down the list of contexts set out below. Consider the following:

- community defined as people in general—this is often the case when the words "the community" are employed. Here "community" is vague and weak.
- community defined as place—this happens when such terms as "a suburban community" or, more specifically, "the Notting Hill

---

[1] See G. A. Hillery, "Definitions of Community: Areas of Agreement", *Rural Sociology* 20:2 (1955), pp. 111–23; T. Blackshaw, *Key Concepts in Community Studies* (London: Sage, 2010).

[2] David Clark, "The Concept of Community—a Re-examination", *The Sociological Review* 21:3 (1973); *Community Education: Towards a Framework for the Future* (Birmingham: Westhill College, 1989).

community" or the like are employed. Here "community" is more specific but only gains strength because of its association with the particular neighbourhood indicated.

- community defined by a common interest—for example, when such terms as "a fishing community" or "the scientific community" are used. Here "community" points to bonds created by shared working or leisure interests, but their strength is undisclosed.
- community defined primarily as relationships—as when phrases like "an Irish community" or "the Asian community" are used. Here the strength of "community" relies on how cohesive the culture of the social collective with which it is associated is assumed to be.

However, to these contextual uses of community, sociologists have added another which raises the concept above the trivial and commonplace to one that is extremely important. This is the context which refers to people's feelings or experience, as when the phrase "a sense of community" is used. From a sociological perspective, this is potentially the concept of community at its most powerful.

Community as feeling

MacIver and Page identify three key aspects or components of community as feeling.[3] These are the feelings engendered when people experience:

- **A sense of security**—having "a place to stand". This is about people feeling physically and materially secure—such as being freed from hunger or violence.
- **A sense of significance**—having "a role to play". This is about people having a sense of self-worth because who they are or what they do is affirmed and validated by those whose opinion they value.

---

[3] In R. M. MacIver and C. H. Page, *Society: An Introductory Analysis* (London: Macmillan, 1950), pp. 291–6. I slightly adapt their terminology.

- **A sense of solidarity**—having "a world to which to belong". This is the feeling which bonds people together within social collectives, from the family to the city, the workplace to the nation.

These experiences together produce the following sociological benchmark:

> The strength of community within any social collective is revealed by the degree to which its members experience a sense of security, of significance and of solidarity.

These three feelings are part of a communal whole and consequently often merge into one another. For example, it is impossible to experience a sense of significance within a group without that spilling over into feeling a sense of solidarity within it. Likewise, it is impossible to feel a sense of solidarity in a group, without that being accompanied by some sense of significance therein. However, MacIver and Page believe that the three feelings identified are sufficiently discrete to make their distinction important for understanding their contribution to a holistic sense of community.

Community as an experience of security, freedom from fear of physical violence or material scarcity of any kind, lays the foundation for a sense of significance and of solidarity to come to the fore. At the same time, all three feelings need to be strong for a collective sense of community to be strong. However, over against Abraham Maslow's "hierarchy of needs" where "self-actualization" (akin to our sense of significance) tops "the pyramid",[4] it is a sense of solidarity that remains the ultimate experiential communal component.

To complete the sociological picture, however, it is necessary to add two other "Ss" at the heart of a developmental process which is essential for the emergence of any sense of community:

---

[4] First suggested by A. H. Maslow, "A theory of human motivation", *Psychological Review* 50:4 (1943), pp. 370–96.

- **Socialization**—the process, in the form of nurture, instruction and training, by means of which people learn to experience and give expression to a sense of security, significance and solidarity.
- **Social control**—that form of authority which normally shapes the socialization process.

"The dark side" of community

Community as feeling is the experiential foundation of human relationships. It has the power to enable relationships to become strong and tenacious. However, community as feeling cannot be the final destination in our quest to build a global community of communities. This is because community as feeling not only has the power to bond collectives together; it has the power to divide and fragment them. In short, community as feeling does not enable us to surmount what earlier I defined as the communal dilemma: *the problem which every social collective faces when the wellbeing of humankind requires that it becomes and remains open to others without undermining its own strength as a community.*

Catholic Social Teaching (CST), as Anna Rowlands reflects, also acknowledges this critical issue. She writes:

> In CST borders are conceived as a relative good and recognized as legitimate only insofar as they protect the common good of the established community and are porous and human, enabling the established community to enact its duty of obligation to offer hospitality and recognize its part in a common good which lies both within and beyond itself.[5]

David Jenkins identifies the communal dilemma very clearly when he writes: "That by which we identify ourselves and have our sense of identity, significance and belonging is also that by which we dehumanize

---

[5] Anna Rowlands, *Towards a Politics of Communion: Catholic Social Teaching in Dark Times* (London: T&T Clark, 2021), p. 83.

others."[6] It is a dilemma which arises from the fact that community as feeling can, by itself, do nothing to prevent human collectives becoming closed, insular and, sometimes, bitter rivals, the very thing that prevents a world in crisis getting its act together. Community constructed only as an affective experience cannot stop human collectives which embody fear of difference, resentment or pride creating rigid and impermeable boundaries around themselves. Human collectives which erect strong and hostile borders, or which deliberately promote a universe of "them" over against "us", may well strengthen a sense of community within their own ranks. However, they do so by devaluing and dehumanizing others. They employ the communal power of "the tribe" to enhance their own identity and wellbeing at the expense of others. They exacerbate human divisions because of their preoccupation with survival or a need to dominate.

No one can doubt that many Germans under the sway of Adolf Hitler experienced a powerful sense of community. Yet an exclusive form of self-serving socialization and rigid racial boundaries led to the dehumanization of Jews and the holocaust. In recent decades, strict boundaries created by the indoctrination of members of al-Qaeda and ISIS have created communities with a very strong sense of security, significance and solidarity. Yet this has been built on the intolerance of any other way of life and led to acts of extreme brutality where "strangers" are concerned. Furthermore, over recent decades, as Tim Marshall reminds us, hopes of building a global community have diminished because an increasing number of nations have built self-protective "walls", physical and cultural, to exclude those whom they regard as incomers or foreigners.[7] As Russia's invasion of Ukraine is demonstrating, community, when defined in experiential and nationalistic terms, is a threat to the wellbeing of humankind.

In all these cases, the affective power of community is being made to serve a worldview of beliefs and values which sets one social collective

---

[6] David Jenkins, *The Contradiction of Christianity* (London: SCM Press, 1976), pp. 14–16.

[7] T. Marshall, *Divided: Why we're living in an age of walls* (London: Elliott & Thompson, 2018).

over against another. In the case of Nazi Germany, it was the belief in the superiority of the Aryan race that turned community into an exclusive concept and a power for evil. In the case of Vladimir Putin and Patriarch Kirill, head of the Russian Orthodox Church, it is the conviction, as the former has stated, that "Ukraine is an inalienable part of our own history, culture and spiritual space",[8] that has led to war.

It is interesting to note here that, with regards to Catholic Social Teaching, Anna Rowlands identifies a similar dilemma which exists in relation to the "dark side" of the concept of "the common good".[9] She argues that there is a long history of the idea of the common good (as with the concept of community) being used "to justify repression, extermination and personal sacrifice in the name of the collectivity" concerned. She continues:

> The idea of the common good is no more immune, *a priori*—in *either* secular *or* religious guise—to integration into a set of exclusive ethno-nationalist claims that, as Pius XI notes, risk raising race, nation or politics beyond 'their standard value' and turning them into forms of death-dealing idolatry.

Nevertheless, the way to surmount the dark side of community and the communal dilemma is not to jettison the concept of community simply because its power can be used to aggrandize, divide and destroy. The way ahead is to embrace a worldview of beliefs and values which have the potential to liberate and harness that power and build an open and inclusive world thereby facilitating the survival and flourishing of humankind.[10]

---

[8] In a speech two days before Russia's invasion of Ukraine.
[9] Rowlands, *Towards a Politics of Communion*, p. 117.
[10] See R. Plant, *Community and Ideology: An Essay in Applied Social Philosophy* (London: Routledge and Kegan Paul, 1974).

3

A Christian symbolic universe

Symbolic universes

Any worldview, be it espoused for good or ill, sociologists Berger and Luckmann call a "symbolic universe".[1] A symbolic universe "integrates different provinces of meaning", including beliefs and values, maxims and customs, signs and rituals, roles and relationships, into a totality which gives purpose and credibility to human society. However, it is the specific beliefs and values espoused which give identity, credibility and ultimate legitimation to whatever "whole (new) world is created".[2]

Every symbolic universe requires "legitimation", some acknowledged authority which "justifies the institutional order by giving normative dignity to its practical imperatives".[3] Legitimation of the symbolic universe depends on an authority which ensures that everything can be taken to be "in its right place"[4] and is functioning to sustain the whole. Legitimation at lower and more operational levels of a symbolic universe is often a responsibility bestowed on symbolic figures, commonly revered as "authorities" or "specialists", who are publicly acknowledged to represent and uphold the beliefs, values and norms of the symbolic universe concerned.

From the perspective of the sociology of community, whatever beliefs and values give meaning and legitimation to a particular symbolic

---

[1] P. Berger and T. Luckmann, *The Social Construction of Reality* (Harmondsworth: Penguin, 1966, 1984), pp. 110–46.

[2] Berger and Luckmann, *The Social Construction of Reality*, p. 114.

[3] Berger and Luckmann, *The Social Construction of Reality*, p. 111.

[4] Berger and Luckmann, *The Social Construction of Reality*, p. 116.

universe will determine for what societal purpose and institutional ends the power of community (deriving from a sense of security, significance and solidarity and the processes of socialization and social control) is being harnessed. If those values and beliefs are inward-looking and narcissistic, the power of community will give impetus to a symbolic universe which is closed, exclusive and divisive. If they are empathetic and outward-looking, what Miroslav Volf calls "other embracing",[5] the power of community will help to bring into being a symbolic universe which is open and inclusive.

Because the kind of symbolic universe described by Berger and Luckmann is "socially constructed", the kind of society and its institutions[6] that shape it are always open to change. This accords with the views of David Graeber and David Wengrow, whose research into those societies which existed before recorded history shows that they were of greatly varying sizes and, of special note, were able to adapt their social structures, for example from hierarchy to collectivity and back again, in order to meet the shifting needs of their members *and* a wider cultural environment.[7]

One lesson to be learnt from this, Graeber and Wengrow argue, is that "complex systems don't have to be organized top-down, either in the natural or in the social world".[8] It also means that the assumption of some anthropologists and historians that human civilization has inevitably changed from the simple to the complex, from the informal to the formal or from the corporate to the hierarchical, and that the latter of these forms are now here to stay, is mistaken. The conclusion of Graeber and Wengrow is that human beings remain free to choose the kind of symbolic universe and the nature of its institutions, be the latter

---

[5] Miroslav Volf, *Exclusion and Embrace: A theological exploration of identity, otherness and reconciliation* (Nashville, TN: Abingdon Press, 2019).

[6] I define an institution as "an established organization which embodies the key functions, values and norms of a society as an enduring social, cultural and economic entity".

[7] D. Graeber and D. Wengrow, *The Dawn of Everything: A New History of Humanity* (London: Allen Lane, 2021).

[8] Graeber and Wengrow, *The Dawn of Everything*, p. 515.

secular or religious, even if any change of symbolic universe takes some time. Consequently, though humankind may feel it is locked for ever into the kind of symbolic universe and form of its institutions which currently dominate the scene, this is not the case. Choosing to adopt a new form of symbolic universe and the institutions shaped by it always remains an option.

Over the centuries, numerous symbolic universes have shaped, and continue to shape, the history of the West. However, it is my contention that there is compelling evidence that the one with the greatest potential for the creation of a global community of communities is that which I describe as "the kingdom community", a symbolic universe representing the embodiment and incarnation of Christian faith. I believe that this symbolic universe is what Tom Holland, in his insightful analysis of "the Western mind", is referring to when he writes of the distinctiveness of the Christian legacy which has permeated the whole of Western culture.[9] Catholic Social Teaching takes a similar view. Anna Rowlands writes:

> What the (papal) encyclicals propose is that . . . the way we trade, eat, house and clothe ourselves are all interconnected by both sets of cultural ideas as well as by political and economic structures. And for most of us in the Northern Hemisphere and Western societies, these ideas even when they appear to be largely secular, often have identifiable Christian roots.[10]

However, because that legacy is now built into the life of the West, its origins are often forgotten and its potential for bringing into being a communally strong *and* inclusive world is in great danger of being lost.

I believe that to meet the crises now facing humankind, it is imperative that we rediscover, re-affirm and build on that Christian legacy. It is a legacy which offers:

---

[9] Tom Holland, *Dominion: The Making of the Western Mind* (London: Abacus, 2019).
[10] Anna Rowlands, *Towards a Politics of Communion: Catholic Social Teaching in Dark Times* (London: T&T Clark, 2021), p. 271.

- **a vision of a Christian symbolic universe** already here and of lasting significance. Such a universe has two complementary components. First, that of a Trinitarian sovereign, who exercises authority over that universe and gives it legitimation. Second, of a people who, in partnership with their sovereign, form "a kingdom community" representing community at its zenith.
- **an experience of a kingdom community which offers humankind its gifts.** These are gifts of grace. They are universal and inclusive.
- **a power to make that vision a reality.** This is the dynamism of the kingdom community's gifts experienced through the rich heritage of Christian worship and Christian spirituality down the ages. It is a power discovered within and beyond the life of the church.
- **a means of communal transformation.** A process by which a communal society and world, inspired by the vision of the kingdom community and empowered by its gifts, can come into being.
- **the nature and form of "sacred" and "secular"**[11] **social collectives** within a Christian symbolic universe.
- **a church which is the servant of the kingdom community and of humankind** and thus a "diaconal" church. It is a church which celebrates, nurtures, discerns and bears witness to the gifts of the kingdom community already present in the world.

I explore all these features of a Christian symbolic universe and its embodiment in the kingdom community more fully in the rest of this book.

The West's right to offer its Christian legacy?
An important issue needs to be addressed here before we move on. It may be that the West has inherited a Christian legacy which, as Tom Holland sees it, is of profound spiritual and ethical importance for the wider

---

[11] I use these terms in their popular sense of that which acknowledges or sets aside the presence of the divine within society.

world.[12] However, what grounds has the West to argue that this legacy is key for the creation of a global community and what right to offer it as such to the rest of humankind? Furthermore, does this mean that other symbolic universes, sacred or secular, some much more historic than Christianity, have nothing to offer the quest for community?

The nations of Europe, and not least Britain, have in past centuries done immense harm (even if making some contribution) to the way of life of the indigenous populations of notably Latin America, Africa and India through their imperialistic ambitions. The slave trade is symbolic of many examples of a misuse of power and of other peoples being abused in order to enrich the West. Furthermore, their indigenous culture was often all but destroyed and the Western way of life, including the beliefs and religious practices of the church of that day, forcibly imposed on them by emerging empires. Only in relatively recent times have these countries begun to throw off an alien culture and reclaim their own cultural and religious heritage.

My response to this historic failure is that the Christian legacy of the West with which Tom Holland is concerned, and the interpretation of the Christian symbolic universe which this book presents, is far removed from the "Christian symbolic universe" represented by the imperialistic designs of many European nations, especially from the eighteenth to early twentieth centuries. During that period the mainstream churches were closely aligned with the dominating culture of the nation concerned and the socialization process related to it. Consequently, in the age of empire building, the church rode on the shoulders of and sought to reinforce the culture of the conquerors.

Over against that situation, I hope what I set out below concerning the nature of a Christian symbolic universe, expressed through the phenomenon of the kingdom community as its practical expression, demonstrates community at its zenith in *any* cultural, religious or social context. In short, my claim is that from a *communal* perspective, what this Western Christian legacy, akin to that of which Tom Holland writes, offers to the wider world is the deepest and richest experience and understanding of *community* available to all. That the West has neglected

---

[12] Holland, *Dominion*.

or distorted this genuine Christian legacy through self-aggrandisement, power-seeking and imperialism is a matter of shame and failure of responsibility, but not of any final judgement on that legacy.

In response to the second question concerning the contribution to a new world order of other symbolic universes, it is quite clear that from the earliest times and down the centuries, many of those espousing such universes have lived their lives in accord with the most positive aspects of the West's Christian legacy.[13] "The golden rule", for example, characterizes all the world's major religious traditions. However, my contention remains that a Christian symbolic universe, which embraces the gifts of a universal and inclusive kingdom community, remains the most holistic expression of community, divine and human, ever offered to humankind.

Tom Holland points to many significant figures and notable events which have contributed to "the making of the Western mind". However, his identification of the West's genuine Christian legacy takes more the form of a series of short historical narratives than a comprehensive and coherent model of the major components of that inheritance. I describe below what I believe to be that same legacy, but as a vision of a Christian symbolic universe embodied in the life of the kingdom community.

---

[13] See Graeber and Wengrow, *The Dawn of Everything*, who argue for the communal quality of life of many early indigenous collectives.

4

The kingdom community

The demise of a kingdom theology

Writing in the mid-1980s, Mortimer Arias bemoans "the eclipse of the kingdom".[1] He argues that "the kingdom-of-God theme has practically disappeared from evangelistic preaching and has been ignored by traditional 'evangelism'". Nor has that theme been clearly in evidence in the West since that time. There would seem to be a number of reasons for this.

One of these is that over recent decades the numerical decline of the mainstream churches in the West has moved from a matter of statistics to a concern about survival. Consequently, the issue of church growth has come increasingly to dominate the councils and synods of the church giving impetus to the increasing domination of an evangelical theology which prioritizes "making disciples" and "planting" new churches. If the term "kingdom" does appear it is, in practice, often interpreted as a synonym for church.

At the same time, as the imperial era of the late nineteenth and early twentieth century has become a matter of history, the concept of monarchy has become largely outdated and the advocacy of women's rights moved to the fore, the term "kingdom" has for many become increasingly anachronistic.

One popular response has been to substitute the word "kin-ship" for kingdom. The difficulty is that "kinship" has a very different meaning from kingdom and that, if hyphenated, is not a recognizable concept.

---

[1] Mortimer Arias, *Announcing the Reign of God: Evangelization and the Subversive Memory of Jesus* (Philadelphia: Fortress Press, 1984), pp. 12 and xv.

From the point of view of biblical scholarship, the obvious way forward is to keep faith with the meaning of the Greek word *basileia* translated as the reign or rule of God. Unfortunately, this term too retains monarchial connotations. Furthermore, it makes no reference to the purpose, nature and form that "citizenship" of such a kingdom should take, individually or collectively.

For lack of a better alternative, therefore, I retain the word "kingdom". However, I add the all-important word "community" which I believe balances and transforms the meaning and nature of kingdom as I seek to show below.

A theology for a time of crisis

The "eclipse of the kingdom" (Arias) is no minor matter. Christ's proclamation that "the time is fulfilled, and the kingdom of God is at hand, repent and believe in the gospel" (Mark 1:15) was a radical message for a time of crisis. As C. H. Dodd argues in his study of the parables, Christ was "no generalizing moralist ... but (addressed) himself, there and then, and with the most stringent urgency, to the crisis which his own person and ministry constituted".[2] He believed that only the good news of the kingdom could save his people from eventual disaster. This was to come only a few generations later with the destruction of the temple in Jerusalem, over which city he wept (Luke 19:41-4).

Likewise, I have argued in what has gone before that the potentially terminal crises which now face humankind demand not only a quest for community and the creation of one world but the universal affirmation of a Christian symbolic universe manifest in the nature and form of the kingdom community. Without the latter "at hand", recognized and affirmed, no institution, be it the church or any other, has the answer to the crises of this millennium. What then are the features and form of this kingdom community?

---

[2] C. H. Dodd, *The Parables of the Kingdom*, revised edn (London: Collins Fount, 1961), p. 8.

A communal theology of the kingdom

The Trinity as sovereign
There can be no kingdom without a "king". The Trinity is the sovereign of the kingdom community because the Trinity is the legitimating authority of a Christian symbolic universe which embodies that community. Just as there has in recent times been "an eclipse of the kingdom", so by the mid-twentieth century the Trinity was being called "the forgotten Trinity".[3] Both urgently need restoration if Christian faith is to make a credible contribution to addressing the crises of our era. However, the nature of Trinitarian authority is all-important.

The Trinity exercises collective authority
The authority exercised by the Trinity is collective in nature and derived from the strength of its communal relationships. The three Persons of the Trinity exercise authority in "collaboration" and "consultation" with one another. Miroslav Volf argues that "in a community of perfect love among persons who share all divine attributes a notion of hierarchy is unintelligible".[4]

The exercise of such collective and non-hierarchical Trinitarian authority challenges what Jürgen Moltmann calls "monotheistic Christianity and Christian monotheism".[5] He writes: "The doctrine of the Trinity which evolves out of the surmounting of monotheism..., must therefore overcome... monarchism, which legitimates dependency, helplessness and servitude."[6] Monarchism of this kind has led to the misguided assumption of the divine right of emperors and kings and the disaster of theocracy. "It is only when the doctrine of the Trinity vanquishes the monotheistic notions of the great universal monarch

---

[3] *The Forgotten Trinity: The BCC Study Commission on Trinitarian Doctrine Today* (London: Churches Together in Britain and Ireland, 2011).

[4] Miroslav Volf, *Exclusion and Embrace: A theological exploration of identity, otherness and reconciliation* (Nashville, TN: Abingdon Press, 2019), p. 350.

[5] Jürgen Moltmann, *The Trinity and Kingdom of God*, tr. Margaret Kohl (London: SCM Press, 1981), p. 191.

[6] Moltmann, *Trinity and the Kingdom of God*, p. 192.

in heaven and his divine patriarchs in the world, that earthly rulers, dictators and tyrants cease to find any justifying religious archetypes any more."[7]

The Trinity exemplifies community at its zenith

Moltmann describes the nature of this "marvellous community" and the implications of its communal essence for humankind and for "the integrity of creation".[8] He writes:

> Even when we simply hear the name of 'the Father, Son and Holy Spirit', we sense that the divine mystery is a marvellous community. The triune God . . . is a God in community, rich in relationships. 'God is love' . . . . If that is true, then we correspond to God not through domination and subjugation but through community and relationships which further life. It is not the solitary human subject who is God's image on earth; it is the true human community. It is not separate, individual parts of creation that reflect God's wisdom and his triune livingness; it is the community of creation as a whole.

At the same time, each person of the Trinity, God, Son and Holy Spirit, possesses a unique identity, their work being accomplished through what might be called a divine "division of labour". Volf writes:

> The life of God is a self-giving and other-receiving love. As a consequence, the identity of each trinitarian person cannot be defined apart from the other persons . . . Every divine person *is* the other persons, but he is the other persons in his own particular way.[9]

---

[7] Moltmann, *The Trinity and Kingdom of God*, p. 197.
[8] Jürgen Moltmann, *God for a Secular Society*, tr. Margaret Kohl (London: SCM Press, 1999), p. 101.
[9] Volf, *Exclusion and Embrace*, p. 129.

"The three divine persons have everything in common, except their personal characteristics", writes Moltmann.[10] Yet "mutual indwelling and reciprocal interpenetration ... bring out the unique unity of the triune God",[11] the consequence being a divine synergy.

The Trinity as analogy

There have been serious challenges posed to the construct of "the social Trinity", not least that it is naive to believe that human beings can "define" the Trinity's nature and form and then assume that certain types of human organization and leadership gain credibility from such definitions. However, whilst recognizing that such assumptions can be seen as claiming validity for what can only be speculation, I argue, with Volf, that "social analogies are indispensable when thinking about the trinity of the one God (and) that without social analogies we could not express something essential about God".[12]

Nevertheless, I believe that, in that quest, the contribution of the Trinity as a communal analogy must be empirically tested. I agree with Volf that "the conceptualization work cannot proceed simply from above (Trinity) to below (church and society)".[13] He argues that "the conceptual construction of the correspondence (of the Trinity to social reality) must go back and forth on a two-way street, both from above and from below".[14] In the context of previous chapters, this means that disciplines such as sociology must inform and "test out" theology, as well as vice versa.

"Citizens" of the kingdom community

There can be no kingdom without a people.

---

[10] Moltmann, *The Trinity and the Kingdom of God*, p. 198.
[11] Jürgen Moltmann, *Ethics of Hope*, tr. Margaret Kohl (Minneapolis, MN: Fortress Press, 2012), p. 137.
[12] Volf, *Exclusion and Embrace*, p. 325.
[13] Volf, *Exclusion and Embrace*, p. 323.
[14] Volf, *Exclusion and Embrace*, p. 347.

The Trinity and the people of God

"The unity of the Christian community is a trinitarian unity", states Jürgen Moltmann.[15] A partnership between the Trinity and humankind remains on offer to all who strive to make the kingdom community manifest in daily life. The implications of that partnership are encapsulated in the extraordinary affirmation of and commission to those who seek the coming of the kingdom community set out in 1 Peter (2:9–10):

> You are a chosen race, a royal priesthood, a holy nation, God's own people, that you may declare the wonderful deeds of him who called you out of darkness into his marvellous light. Once you were no people but now you are God's people; once you had not received mercy but now you have received mercy.

Consequently, as Moltmann puts it: "The hierarchy which preserves and enforces unity is replaced by the brotherhood and sisterhood of the community of Christ."[16]

Christ called his followers his "friends" and identified them as his partners. As he stated: "You did not choose me, but I chose you and appointed you that you should go and bear fruit and that your fruit should abide" (John 15:16). It was a partnership first in evidence when he sent out his disciples on mission, and when he delivered his final commission to the eleven (Matthew 28:18–20). That partnership was given new impetus on the Day of Pentecost and shared by an ever-widening band of followers during New Testament times. It has been a partnership entered into by many millions down the centuries.

The Trinity's power to surmount the communal dilemma

That the Trinity is "a community within a kingdom community" demonstrates its power to surmount the communal dilemma, in human affairs a dilemma typified by the fear of what John Zizioulas calls

---

[15] Moltmann, *The Trinity and the Kingdom of God*, p. 202.
[16] Moltmann, *The Trinity and the Kingdom of God*, p. 202.

"otherness".[17] He argues that "the unbreakable *koinonia* (community) that exists between the three Persons . . . means that otherness is not a threat to unity but the *sine qua non* of it". He contends that " . . . there is no other model for the proper relation between communion and otherness either for the Church or for the human being (sic) than the Trinitarian God". Divine openness and inclusiveness embrace not only friends but strangers, and even "enemies", as Christ's words from the cross demonstrated (Luke 23:34). Such openness and inclusiveness multiply and disseminate, they do not attenuate or dissipate the gifts which the Trinity offers humankind.

The Trinity legitimates and empowers the people of God to surmount the communal dilemma and create one world. As the doxology to the Lord's Prayer states, "(God's) is the kingdom, the power and the glory". Or, as one adaptation of the Lord's Prayer puts it, God's is "a power which never crushes and a glory which never dazzles".[18] Such power is inexhaustible. It is shown through compassion and affirmation, not by domination, cruelty, repression or retribution. It is a power which permeates and energizes the gifts of the kingdom community identified below. It is offered to all who respond positively to the Trinity's call to become partners in the task of building the kingdom community.

The gifts of the kingdom community

The kingdom as a community offers humanity five core gifts—those of life, liberation, love, learning and servant leadership. It is imperative to recognize that these gifts build on yet transform the five primary sociological components of community identified earlier—a sense of security, significance and solidarity, and the process of socialization and social control. *These five primary sociological components of community form the experiential foundations of the theological gifts of the kingdom community.* However, their theological counterparts are essential in

---

[17] In Paul M. Collins, *The Trinity: A Guide for the Perplexed* (London: T&T Clark, 2008), p. 124.

[18] David Clark, *The Lord's Prayer* (2008, unpublished prayers).

transforming, deepening and universalizing that sociological experience, thereby offering an understanding of community at its zenith. The giver of the gifts of the kingdom community, their legitimatizing authority, and the source of their power is the Trinity.

I note below the sociological underpinning and their Trinitarian source. Moltmann offers a somewhat similar association of the persons of the Trinity with the first three gifts.[19] I offer brief examples of the biblical underpinning of these gifts.[20]

- **The gift of life** (transforming a sense of *security*)—is offered by God as Creator. "For with you is the fountain of life ... " (Psalm 36:9).
- **The gift of liberation** (transforming a sense of *significance*)—is offered by Christ as Liberator. (Christ said:) "(The Lord) has appointed me to preach good news to the poor. He has sent me to proclaim release to the captives and recovering of sight to the blind, to set at liberty those who are oppressed" (Luke 4:18).
- **The gift of love** (transforming a sense of *solidarity*)—is offered by the Holy Spirit as Unifier. (Paul wrote:) "The fruit of the Spirit is love ... " (Galatians 5:22).
- **The gift of learning** (transforming the experience of *socialization*)—is bestowed by the Trinity as a learning community. Christ was concerned that his followers engage in learning for life. This meant learning not only how to fulfil their own human potential, but how to live and work together as a community; in short, how to put into practice the other gifts of the kingdom community. Christ encouraged his listeners to re-examine their values, as in the case of Sunday observance (Mark 2:23–8; 3:1–6), to question the importance of wealth (Mark 10:17–31; Luke 12:13–21), to review their response to the faults of others and, most challenging of all, to reflect on how they treated their enemies (Matthew 5:38–42,43–8).

---

[19] Moltmann, *The Trinity and the Kingdom of God*, pp. 209–12.
[20] See also Appendix 1.

- **The gift of servant leadership** (transforming the experience of *social control*)—exemplified by the life and ministry of Christ. (Christ said:) "... whoever would be great among you must be your servant, and whoever would be first among you must be your slave; even as the Son of Man came not to be served but to serve, and to give his life as a ransom for many" (Matthew 20:26–8). (Paul wrote:) "Have this mind among yourselves, which you have in Christ Jesus, who, though he was in the form of God, did not count equality with God a thing to be grasped, but emptied himself, taking the form of a servant, being born in the likeness of men" (Philippians 2:5–7).

Although the source of the power of these gifts of the kingdom community can be associated with different persons of the Trinity, our understanding of the nature of that community is pre-eminently seen in the life of Christ. As Lesslie Newbigin put it: "The news is that 'the kingdom of God' is no longer a theological phrase. There is now a name and a human face (to put to it)", that of Jesus Christ.[21] It is in his person, his ministry, life, death and resurrection that the kingdom community has been made incarnate. He becomes what I later describe as "the symbolic person" who draws together a band of disciples and initiates a new movement for the communal transformation of humankind.

- The gifts of the kingdom community are just that—"pure gift".[22] Their source is the Trinity which is alone the giver and sustainer of the richness and power of these blessings.
- The gifts of the kingdom community are offered first and foremost to the weakest in society, not because they are to be pitied but because they have pride of place in that community. Christ gave "priority in the announcement of the kingdom to the poor, the

---

[21] Lesslie Newbigin, *Your Kingdom Come* (Leeds: John Paul, The Preacher's Press, 1980), p. 20.
[22] Newbiggin, *Your Kingdom Come*, p. 23.

outcasts, the marginals, the 'little ones,' the sick, the despised and the rejected—the sinned-against".[23]

As with the experiential sentiments of a sociological understanding of community (a sense of security, significance and solidarity), the gifts of the kingdom community (life, liberation, love and learning) are complementary. *The gifts of life* and *liberation* animate and free us to experience *the gift of love* (1 Corinthians 13). *Learning* is the gift which enables us to engage in a journey of spiritual discovery, not least to discover the deepest meaning of the kingdom community and the source of its power.

The gifts of the kingdom community are *inclusive* and *universal*. They operate in all situations: the kingdom of God is "in our midst" (Luke 17:21), whether or not its presence is recognized. At the same time, all these gifts, like that of love, "*abide*" (1 Corinthians 13:13 and 8); that is, they never fail. They are ongoing, as the message of Easter declares, this side of mortality and beyond. They surmount the temporality of any sociological construction of community.

Attributes of the gifts of the kingdom community

It is significant that much of what we know about the nature of the kingdom has come to us through the stories or parables which Christ told, the message of which was lived out in Christ's own words and deeds. The parables show that the kingdom is not some remote theological concept, but something rooted in the real world, their predominant focus being the everyday concerns of ordinary people and the lessons of nature.

At the same time, many of the parables of the kingdom, though at times seemingly simple and domestic, are profoundly counter-cultural.[24] They are stories which encourage the listener to question ethical norms and religious practices, and to discover the practical implications of being associated with the kingdom.

---

[23] Arias, *Announcing the Reign of God*, p. 79.

[24] Dodd, *Parables of the Kingdom*.

Christ's life and work, and his parables of the kingdom, indicate that each gift has additional attributes which broaden and enrich it.[25] These would include:

- Life—Security (its sociological component); health; vitality; creativity; care of the planet.
- Liberation—Significance (its sociological component); human dignity; equality; justice—restorative; justice—distributive; forgiveness; reconciliation.
- Love—Solidarity (its sociological component); compassion; empathy; caring; sharing; generosity.
- Learning—Socialization (its sociological component); a quest for truth; attention; openness; questioning assumptions; person-centred learning.
- Servant leadership—Social control (its sociological component); visionary; strategist; catalyst; intermediary; enabler; educator; partner.

The meaning of each of these attributes, and of the gifts of the kingdom community with which they are associated, needs to be explored at greater depth than is possible in this book. However, I begin this process in Chapter 4. I also refer to these attributes again when identifying symbolic figures, groups, movements and organizations which appear to manifest these gifts in today's world. I spell out more practically the associated roles of servant leadership when considering the ministry of the diaconal church in Chapter 9.

Among other important contributions to a deeper understanding and appreciation of the meaning and implications of these attributes of the gifts of the kingdom community is Catholic Social Teaching. As Anna Rowlands shows, the latter has a good deal of wisdom to offer concerning a number of these attributes. For example, with regards to human dignity (associated with the gift of liberation) she refers to John

---

[25] See Appendix 1 for biblical references relating to these attributes. See also *The Kingdom at Work Project: A Handbook*, pp. 24–8. Obtainable in digital form from rev.julian.e.blakemore@gmail.com.

Milbank who reminds us of "the secular tendencies to frame dignity in a form of liberal individualism that is fundamentally tied to modern capitalism",[26] rather than it being recognized as a God-given status and thus a core component of what it means to be fully human, individually and collectively.

The attribute of solidarity (associated with the gift of love) is also one which looms large in Catholic Social Teaching. Anna Rowlands records how its meaning has developed over the history of papal encyclicals.[27] The term is defined by Rowlands as "a structural orientation towards ensuring the dignity and development of the human person"[28] and has a rich history. However, even in Catholic Social Teaching the meaning of the term remains so all-embracing that Pope Francis can regard it "as an increasingly 'dirty' word, seen as naïve and worn".[29] This leads Francis to use other terms, such as "fraternity",[30] to elucidate it. However, Rowlands notes that in CST there is a crucially important acknowledgement that solidarity must extend *across* social and cultural boundaries if it is not to foster an incestuous experience.[31]

All these attributes, though needing clear and communally creative exposition, are highly relevant to the needs of a world in crisis, because they help to reveal with greater clarity the deeper meaning of the foundational Trinitarian communal gifts of life, liberation, love, learning and servant leadership.

The kingdom community and communal wholeness

Though the gifts of the kingdom community and their attributes are here presented as distinctive components of the kingdom community, in practice together they form a communal entity in which the whole is greater than the sum of the parts. That whole is a glimpse into the divine mystery of community at its zenith. It is a profound encounter with what

---

[26] Rowlands, *Towards a Politics of Communion*, p. 69.

[27] Rowlands, *Towards a Politics of Communion*, pp. 239–67.

[28] Rowlands, *Towards a Politics of Communion*, p. 90.

[29] Rowlands, *Towards a Politics of Communion*, p. 262.

[30] Rowlands, *Towards a Politics of Communion*, p. 264.

[31] Rowlands, *Towards a Politics of Communion*, pp. 249–50.

I call "communal wholeness" or "holiness".[32] It is an experience of human beings at one with the divine which even Christian mystics down the ages have struggled to comprehend. It is an experience of the kingdom community as one of rich diversity within unity, and of unity embracing rich diversity. It is an experience of what it means to be "one in Christ". It is to grasp what it is to be "a chosen race, a royal priesthood, a holy nation, God's own people" (1 Peter 2:9). It is an experience of what, at its fullest, it means to be whole persons, whole groups, whole neighbourhoods, whole movements, whole institutions, whole cities, whole societies, one world and of being part of "the integrity of creation".

Communal worship and spirituality

The communal quality of worship

Christian worship nourishes and empowers all the gifts of the kingdom community.[33] In worship, *the gift of life* is enhanced by adoration, praise and thanksgiving. *The gift of liberation* is experienced in confession and forgiveness. *The gift of love* finds expression notably in the intercessions. *The gift of learning* is furthered by hearing the Word and reflecting on its exposition. Commitment to bearing witness to all these gifts is reinforced by the offertory and prayer of dismissal. *The gift of servant leadership* is often revealed in the conduct of worship as a whole.

In relation to the sacraments, I see the sacrament of baptism as giving profound meaning to *the gifts of life* and *liberation*. The Eucharist for many churches is the focal point of worship. For me, it exemplifies in particular *the gifts of liberation* and *love*. However, it also demonstrates that "the Christian life is essentially and inescapably a corporate life... It is impossible to have Christ without one's neighbour in Christ". At the same time, as John Robinson wrote:

---

[32] David Clark, *Reshaping the Mission of Methodism* (Oldham: Church in the Market Place, 2010), pp. 167–91.

[33] David Clark, *The Kingdom at Work Project* (Peterborough: Upfront Publishing, 2016), pp. 299, 321–3.

> What we receive as we hold out our hands round the table is our *own* share in Christ's death and life, our own involvement in it, which can be ours and no one else's ... It is one of the deep mysteries of the truth as it is in Jesus that there is no contradiction or even antithesis between the personal and the social. The collective may be the antithesis of the individual, but the communal is not the enemy of the personal.[34]

One other feature to note when worship and the sacraments are permeated by the gifts of the kingdom community is that these celebrations are open and inclusive. All are welcome if they come to participate in sincerity and all are equal as they worship. Human status is here replaced by the divine affirmation of human dignity accorded to and shared by each and all.

Communal spiritualities

Christian spiritualities which throughout history have deepened and personalized the meaning of the gifts of the kingdom community and offered ways of putting them into practice are another invaluable resource.

For example, I argue elsewhere that Celtic spirituality[35] embodies and enriches *the gift of life*: "The God whom they (the Celts) worshipped was not conceived primarily as the Lord of history ... but rather as the Lord of Creation, the one who revealed himself most fully and characteristically in the wonders and splendours of the natural world."[36] He was described as "the Craftsman of the Heavens". The Celts believed that they were co-workers with God the Creator: "Everything they touched, every tool they handled, was done with respect and reverence; every activity performed with a sense of the presence of God, indeed done in partnership with him."[37]

---

[34] J. A. T. Robinson, "The meaning of the Eucharist", in *Where Three Ways Meet* (London: SCM Press, 1977), pp. 156–7.

[35] See, for example, Esther de Waal, *The Celtic Way of Prayer* (London: Hodder & Stoughton, 1996).

[36] Clark, *Kingdom at Work Project*, pp. 61–83, here at p. 52.

[37] de Waal, *The Celtic Way of Prayer*, p. 70.

I suggest that Ignatian spirituality enhances *the gift of liberation*. For Ignatius, life was a journey from captivity to liberty. He believed his spiritual *Exercises* should lead to a definitive choice between good and evil. The purpose of the *Exercises* is "the overcoming of self and the ordering of one's life on the basis of a decision made in freedom from any disordered attachment".[38] Ignatius saw the Christian as needing to be liberated from powerful forces which distract human beings from the way of Christ, in order to be able to engage in "effective not affective love".

For John Wesley, the founder of Methodism, all words and deeds resulting from *the gift of love* are "the work of the Holy Spirit".[39] For Wesley, the Spirit working within us offers to the whole of humankind not only the assurance of sins forgiven, but the passion to live out our liberation by witnessing to the transforming nature of the love of God. This experience Wesley described as a "religion of the heart".

I see *the gift of learning* as the foundation of Quaker spirituality.[40] It is a gift which creates and enriches the Society of Friends as a learning community. The witness of the Society is rooted in the conviction that Quakers are called to a life-long journey of spiritual discovery. Quakers believe that their experience as a learning community must be made manifest in every aspect of life. Quakers should "seek to understand the causes of injustice, social unrest and fear". Their learning needs to "bear witness to the humanity of all people" and help create "a just and compassionate society".

---

[38] *The Spiritual Exercises of Saint Ignatius Loyola*, tr. G. Hughes and M. Ivens (Leominster: Gracewing, 2004), para. 21, p. 11.

[39] C. Williams, *John Wesley's Theology Today* (London: Epworth Press, 1960), p. 100.

[40] See *Quaker Faith and Practice (QFP)* (London: Religious Society of Friends, 3rd edn, 2005).

Models of the kingdom

What I have presented in this section of the book can be described as a "model of the kingdom". Howard Snyder in his book *Models of the Kingdom* states that models "are often the lenses through which we view reality".[41] He argues that in speaking about the concept of the kingdom, some model is always implicit. What matters is whether it helps to inform and clarify rather than confuse or distort.

Models, whether of the kingdom or church, have come into their own as a response to the increasing pluralization and globalization of society and world. They help us to distinguish between different constructions or interpretations of the same phenomenon. In the case of the kingdom, our challenge is to decide which model accords most fully with our Christian heritage, including its biblical roots, and is also of most relevance to the needs of our age.

Snyder describes nine "models of the kingdom". These regard the kingdom as primarily "a future hope"; an "inner spiritual experience"; "a mystical communion"; a "countersystem"; a "political state"; a "Christianized culture"; an "earthly utopia"; or as "Christian faithfulness". He believes each of these has something of value to contribute to our understanding of the kingdom. However, an issue to which I return later in this book, he believes that a misguided approach is to equate the kingdom with "the institutional church". This abrogates to the church an authority and function which has often entrenched rather than surmounted what I describe as the communal dilemma, exacerbating religious divides and undermining the impact of the church's mission.

There is a great deal of value in Snyder's analysis of different models of the kingdom. However, I believe that the model of *the kingdom community* not only meets all the criteria which he argues must be in place to meet the challenge of authenticity but has particular relevance to "the state we're in". The model of the kingdom community is grounded in the life and teaching of Christ, is at the heart of the experience of the early church, accords with the riches of the Christian heritage which Tom

---

[41] H. A. Snyder, *Models of the Kingdom* (Eugene, OR: Wipf & Stock, 2001, previously published by Abingdon Press, 1991), p. 11.

Holland argues has been bequeathed to the West, is of crucial importance to the communal needs of a world in crisis and has a strong empirical foundation in the social sciences.[42]

"The beloved community"

The concept of the kingdom community is not entirely new. It is implicit, and sometimes explicit, in most of Snyder's models. However, the model most akin to it was adopted to striking effect, though with a slightly different name, "the beloved community", by Martin Luther King in his pursuit of civil rights for the black population of the United States in the 1950s and 1960s. King took this concept from the work of the philosopher Josiah Royce but gave it a new and powerful empirical dynamic.

King's commitment to the beloved community grew out of his involvement with the Montgomery bus boycott by the town's black population in the mid-1950s. It became the motivating vision of his fight for civil rights over the next decade. His belief, as with ours relating to the kingdom community as being imperative for humankind, was similar: "Now the judgment of God is upon us, and we must learn together as brothers or we are all going to perish as fools."[43] The logic of King's dream was theologically specific: "Beloved community as the realization of divine love in lived social relations."[44] That love he identified as *agape*: "the outrageous venture of loving the other without conditions—a risk and a costly sacrifice". *Agape* was a divine gift. Emanating from that gift, his vision was one of a world where people of all races, genders, cultures and generations would live together in unity. "The end is reconciliation, the end is redemption", King said, "the end is the creation of the Beloved community".[45] Other key values of the beloved community were justice for all, not only for black citizens, and upholding the principle of

---

[42] T. Holland, *Dominion: The Making of the Western Mind* (London: Abacus, 2019).

[43] Quoted in C. Marsh, *The Beloved Community: How Faith Shapes Social Justice from the Civil Rights Movement to Today* (New York: Basic Books (Perseus), 2005), p. 149.

[44] Marsh, *The Beloved Community*, p. 2.

[45] Marsh, *The Beloved Community*, p. 1.

non-violence. It was a community created and empowered by a God of compassion and justice and not a human achievement.

King saw the beloved community growing out of the church, originally the black churches of Montgomery but soon well beyond: "In other words, the brotherhood and sisterhood of humankind radiates out from the fellowship of the faithful."[46] However, he argued, "as Christians build beloved communities in, through, and outside the church, they must remain humbled by the camaraderie of unbelievers and non-Christians, grateful for their passion, and inspired ... by their pilgrimage in service ...".[47] His vision of the liberating universality of the beloved community was summed up in the concluding words of his famous speech from the Lincoln Memorial in Washington in August 1963:

> ... when we let (freedom) ring from every village and every hamlet, from every state and every city, we will be able to speed up that day when *all* of God's children, black men and white men, Jews and Gentiles, Protestants and Catholics, will be able to join hands and sing in the words of the old Negro spiritual: *Free at last! Free at last! Thank God Almighty, we are free at last!*

King did not explicitly equate the beloved community with the civil rights movement, though others did. However, for him, it remained the vision inspiring that movement, giving momentum to its practical expression through groups of Christians and those of other convictions committed to the values of universal inclusivity. Marsh writes that for King:

> The kingdom grounds, frames, and surrounds the pursuit of beloved community, gives it permanence in eternity, that it never possesses in time (although for the time it remains visible, it opens onto eternity), gives it a memory that sharpens focus, inspires action, and sustains hope.[48]

---

[46] Marsh, *The Beloved Community*, p. 50.
[47] Marsh, *The Beloved Community*, p. 210.
[48] Marsh, *The Beloved Community*, p. 211.

The bonding across old divides which the dream of the beloved community gave to the civil rights movement began to weaken soon after new civil rights legislation in late 1964. The reasons were complex. They included "an emergent black separatism, the mobilization of white student energies toward anti-war activism (and away from racial matters), the burgeoning women's liberation movement, the search for new religious experiences and an alternative consciousness, and the persisting segregationist views of the white church in the South."[49] Martin Luther King himself was assassinated in 1968. Nonetheless, the vision of the beloved community achieved a great deal and has continued to inspire people to this day as Charles Marsh documents.[50] It remains a seminal model for our concept of the kingdom community.

The validity of "building" the kingdom community

Paul Avis argues that "According to the New Testament, one may 'discern' the kingdom, 'receive' the kingdom, 'enter' the kingdom, and rejoice in the kingdom, but never 'build the kingdom' or 'extend the kingdom'".[51] In one sense, he is right. As Mortimer Arias puts it, "The kingdom in Jesus' proclamation is a human experience, but it is not a human construction or a human programme—it is God's gift of grace."[52] The kingdom will always remain miracle and mystery and a gift beyond human understanding. This is why theologians can say that the kingdom has that of what Rudolf Otto calls "the numinous", the holy, about it, and is beyond human comprehension.[53] Therefore, it is argued, for anyone to claim to be able to "build" the kingdom is not only a total fallacy but bordering on blasphemy. It ignores the infinite gulf between God and humanity created by human sinfulness.

---

[49] Marsh, *The Beloved Community*, p. 2.
[50] Marsh, *The Beloved Community*, p. 2.
[51] Paul Avis, *Reconciling Theology* (London: SCM Press, 2022), p. 108.
[52] Arias, *Announcing the Kingdom of God*, p. 16.
[53] Rudolf Otto, *The Idea of the Holy* (Oxford: Oxford University Press, 1968 [1923]).

On the other hand, it is crystal clear that Christ focused his life and teaching on trying to enable ordinary people to grasp what the kingdom was all about. The parables could be, and often were, misunderstood, but they were Christ's attempt to unravel the mysteries of the kingdom and make the latter better understood. He likened the kingdom to treasure in a field which a man found and covered up and a valuable pearl which a merchant was determined to buy at any cost (Matthew 13:44–5). Though the kingdom was extremely precious, it seems that both were in some way able to "possess" it.

I would argue, therefore, that to assert that fallible human beings, aware of their failings and limitations, cannot in any way facilitate "the coming" of the kingdom is to reduce the people of God to dependent and passive subjects. If we are called by Christ to seek and discern the signs of the kingdom (Matthew 6:33), as Avis accepts, we must surely also be called to respond to such discernment in ways which enable that kingdom "to come" more fully. Christ sent out his disciples not only "to preach the kingdom of God" but "to heal" (Luke 9:2), to make the kingdom a reality in people's everyday lives.

Furthermore, Paul designated his people as "fellow workers for the kingdom of God" (Colossians 4:11) and "fellow workers for God ... , God's field, God's building" (1 Corinthians 3:9). We may not be the architects or the building executives of the kingdom, but we can be bricklayers. It is in the sense of being partners with and, indeed, "friends" (John 15:14) of "the king", that, in what follows, I speak of the people of God, and all fellow travellers, as Martin Luther King argued in relation to the beloved community, being commissioned to be co-workers in "building" the kingdom community or "building" kingdom communities.

The kingdom community

A theology of community

Whole persons—whole groups—whole movements
—whole institutions—whole societies—
one world—"the integrity of creation"
"Communal holiness"

The Trinity

Servant leadership

The gift of Life — *God as Creator*
The gift of Liberation — *Christ as Liberator*
The gift of Love — *Holy Spirit as Unifier*

Universal and inclusive
The gift of Learning
Learning as education (open)

Communal transformation

The communal dilemma!

Socialization
Learning as nurture, instruction and training (closed)
Social control

A sense of **Security** — A sense of **Significance** — A sense of **Solidarity**

A sociology of community

5

Building the kingdom community

Institutionalization

The good news concerning the kingdom community was foundational for the ministry of Christ and the life of the early church. Embracing this radical communal vision compelled the early church to seek to change the mores and culture of, first, Judean, then, Roman society and their institutions. I define an institution as: "an established organization which embodies the key functions, values and norms of a society as an enduring social, cultural and economic entity". In short, the mission of the early church was to replace the existing symbolic universes and their institutions, Jewish and Roman, with one which they believed to be Christian.

Changes of symbolic universe and the process of "institutionalization"
It is helpful, at this point, to have an idea of how such a change of symbolic universe, and of the beliefs, values and culture which it embraces, occurs. Such an understanding is especially useful if we are to grasp how the West's Christian legacy, which has taken shape over many centuries, might continue to transform and enrich humankind. Here the process of societal transition which Berger and Luckmann describe as "institutionalization"[1] is very helpful.

---

[1] The process of "institutionalization" is described fully by Peter Berger in Berger and Luckmann, *The Social Construction of Reality* (Harmondsworth: Penguin, 1966, 1984), pp. 65–146. It is a process which has certain affinities with so-called "theories of international relations" as set out for example in

For a symbolic universe to be incorporated into the life of a society, the process of institutionalization becomes paramount.[2] This is because, for Berger and Luckmann, society is an "agglomeration of institutions".[3] It is these institutions which offer society a common heritage, give it continuity and ensure its stability. Institutional mores help to make the nature of socialization clear and acceptable, thus ensuring that each generation can follow naturally in the footsteps of those that have gone before. Because institutions offer members of a society "predefined patterns of conduct"[4] and a range of established roles, patterns of everyday life become taken for granted. This prevents time and energy being expended on undefined and unexpected ways in which people might interact and relate and removes uncertainty and anxiety from human encounters. Institutions help society to experience a strong sense of community by entrenching norms in social structures which are recognized and predictable to all.

Institutions are slow to form. They come into being through an ongoing process of what Berger and Luckmann call "habitualization".[5] The latter refers to similar forms of human interaction repeated again and again in the course of continuing human contact. Over time, these ways of relating become "habitual" or "harden".[6] They accumulate as norms and mores within institutions which represent different societal functions such as family life, education, work, leisure, religious observance, law and order and government. Certain institutions, for example those representing royalty, can also be of great symbolic importance for a society. Because institutions represent set expectations for large bodies of people, they exercise a coercive power within society which makes stepping out of line difficult. Institutions are consequently slow to decline and collapse.

Nevertheless, no institution lasts for ever. As Berger and Luckmann argue, institutions can become less able to shape and control the life of

---

R. Devetak et al. (eds), *Theories of International Relations*, 6th edn (London: Bloomsbury Academic, 2022).

[2] Berger and Luckmann, *The Social Construction of Reality*, pp. 65–109.
[3] Berger and Luckmann, *The Social Construction of Reality*, p. 73.
[4] Berger and Luckmann, *The Social Construction of Reality*, p. 72.
[5] Berger and Luckmann, *The Social Construction of Reality*, pp. 70ff.
[6] Berger and Luckmann, *The Social Construction of Reality*, p. 76.

a society which, amongst other factors, is demographically numerous, gains surplus economic wealth or moves towards an advanced division of labour.[7] They can also fail to adapt to a changing world around them, typical of the modern era. This gives increasing opportunities for new symbolic universes, or secondary sub-universes, to initiate a fresh habitualization and institutionalization process.

Symbolic figures, groups and social movements
One notable way in which an emerging symbolic universe can give impetus to a fresh institutionalization process is through the driving force of symbolic figures, groups and social movements. A symbolic figure (or figures), who personifies, clarifies and gives dynamism to new beliefs and values which are counter-cultural, can in this context be an important trigger. He or she will usually gather a core group or groups around them to promote the new beliefs, values and way of life concerned. Over time, more groups are spawned which network together to form a counter-cultural social movement.

If, through a new habitualization process driven by such a social movement, the beliefs and values generated become widely accepted as normative, a transformation of existing institutions will occur and, if ongoing, bring about an end to the influence of their overarching symbolic universe. In time, however, the emergence of a new symbolic universe will trigger another cycle of institutionalization, although it usually takes some generations to transform an existing social system.

What Berger and Luckmann do not explore is the human cost of such a transformation. Because a new institutionalization process can lead to a radical break with the past, those seeking a change of beliefs, values and norms, as well as those being pressed to accommodate such change, may well find themselves engaged in extended periods of conflict.[8] Nor do Berger and Luckmann address the situation where new forms of institution, and their mores, are forced on a society through external

---

[7] Berger and Luckmann, *The Social Construction of Reality*, pp. 98–9.
[8] See for example Jürgen Moltmann, *The Crucified God: The Cross of Christ as the Foundation and Criticism of Christian Theology*, tr. R. A. Wilson and J. Bowden (London: SCM Press, 1973).

military, economic or related means. However, I believe they would argue that, even in the latter situation, the emergence of any sustained change of beliefs, values and mores, and thus the establishment of a new form of institutionalization, usually takes many years to achieve.

An historical perspective on the West's Christian legacy

From the early church to the Reformation
Here I offer a brief overview of how the institutionalization of a *Christian* symbolic universe has bequeathed the West its Christian legacy. Because I interpret this process as the operationalization of the gifts of the kingdom community, I evaluate it as a process of "*communal* transformation" and, therefore, "*communal* institutionalization". It is also a process of *transformation*, in Paul's sense of the renewal of the mind as well as the heart (Romans 12:2). In the life of the West, it is a process which shows evidence of only partial fulfilment and remains ongoing. Especially in more recent centuries, it is a process which has seen a diversity of other symbolic universes also vying to dominate Western culture.

The early church
The process of communal institutionalization was very much what was witnessed during the first three centuries of the life of the early church. The process began with the emergence of a symbolic figure, Christ, who challenged the religious and cultural status quo to offer a new way of life, a new symbolic universe, the kingdom community (Mark 1:14–15), to the people of his day. He began his ministry by gathering a small group around him who learnt from his teaching and ministry. After his crucifixion and what they believed to be his resurrection, his followers took responsibility for the wider dissemination of his counter-cultural message.

The early Christians formed small cells (churches) which, with the encouragement of other symbolic figures, such as Paul, linked up to form loose networks and then a movement which gave impetus to the emergence of a new and dynamic Christian symbolic universe. After three centuries, which saw many Christians persecuted or martyred in that cause, the movement was given institutional form by the imperial decrees of Emperor Constantine (314), and later Theodosius (380). These produced a radical religious and cultural shift in the life of the Roman Empire. Nevertheless, for many years the way in which the gifts of the kingdom community were manifest remained both shaped and constrained by Roman customs and mores.

Christendom

Following the collapse of the Roman Empire, and after centuries of tribal invasions of Western Europe, a new and more stable world gradually emerged. This was in large part brought about by the process of symbolic figure(s)—groups—movements and "institutionalization" as described above. This time, however, it was a *Christian* symbolic universe which was the dominant driving force.

In that process, the monastic movement, its life strongly influenced by Benedict and his communal Rule, played a crucial role. Indeed, some historians believe that, after the fall of the Roman Empire, it was the monastic movement which preserved the Christian faith from extinction.[9] The outcome was the creation from AD 800 onwards of a "New Roman Empire",[10] with the Carolingian dynasty dominant and its institutions formally shaped by Christian values, norms and rituals.[11] Ultimate religious authority came to be vested in the papacy. By the tenth century, Latin (or Western) Christendom had emerged, bringing with it an ongoing struggle for supremacy between Emperor and Pope.

Another symbolic universe, that of Islam, appeared on the scene from the seventh century onwards. However, it never penetrated Western Europe beyond Spain where, in time, Christian and Muslim cultures often existed peacefully side-by-side. Islam as a religion made few significant inroads into Christendom. However, it did make notable scientific, philosophical, medical and artistic contributions to Western

---

[9] For example, Diarmaid MacCulloch, *A History of Christianity* (London: Allen Lane, 2009), p. 358.

[10] MacCulloch, *A History of Christianity*, pp. 346–62.

[11] MacCulloch, *A History of Christianity*, pp. 346–62.

thinking and culture. It also brought economic enrichment, notably through opening up new trading opportunities.

As a new symbolic universe, Christendom enabled a large constituency to experience the kingdom community's gift of love, especially through the ordinary routines of daily life and worship.[12] However, the gift of life was inevitably circumscribed by the material and physical hazards of the age. Understanding of the gift of liberation was hampered by a belief in the primacy of divine retributive justice and the threat of eternal punishment. The gift of learning was circumscribed by Christendom's closed systems of socialization and social control. Servant leadership was hampered by rigid hierarchies, sacred (papal) and secular (feudal), and the frequent rivalries which they engendered.

Nevertheless, Larry Siedentop believes that during the later centuries of Christendom, especially amongst the intellectual élite, Christian faith enabled "the Western mind" to begin to recognize and affirm the dignity of the individual and the "moral equality" of humankind, important attributes of the gift of liberation. These developments, Siedentop writes, "make it the gateway to modern Europe" emphasizing "the rightful claims of conscience and civil liberty (and) ... the importance of government by consent".[13]

The Protestant Reformation

This religious "liberation movement" slowly gained momentum throughout the West from the mid-fourteenth century onwards, John Wycliffe (1328–84) being regarded as its "morning star". However, its international "launch" is normally associated with Martin Luther making his "95 theses" public in 1517. The Reformation soon became a new form of Christian symbolic universe and institutional expression of Christian faith. Symbolic figures, such as Martin Luther, John Calvin and Huldrych Zwingli, gave impetus to fundamental theological and social change, with the gifts of liberation and learning to the fore. The

---

[12] See Eamon Duffy, *The Stripping of the Altars: Traditional Religion in England 1400–1580*, 2nd edn (London: Yale University Press, 2005).

[13] Larry Siedentop, *Inventing the Individual: The Origins of Western Liberalism* (London: Allen Lane, 2014), p. 306.

individual(s)—group(s)—movement—institutionalization process again gave momentum to profound cultural, social and religious change.

At the same time, the Reformation was instrumental in the fragmentation of Christendom into a wide diversity of religious movements, some in the centuries ahead leading to the creation of prominent denominational institutions. The emerging churches broke fresh ground in affirming and embracing the gift of liberation, though most remained closed to and dismissive of others' claim to "the truth". Though new universities and public schools, as well as the coming of the printing press, enabled many to begin to question the religious status quo, the gift of learning was still limited to an educational élite and by closed forms of socialization.[14] The potential for servant leadership remained unrealized, competing sacred (clerical) and secular (royal and military) hierarchies of social control remaining normative. In this sense, many characteristics of the culture of Christendom lived on, though the earlier homogeneity and conformity of the Western church would never return. As far as the gift of life was concerned, for many their existence remained "nasty, brutish and short".

Post-Reformation to the First World War
The centuries since the Reformation have seen the emergence in the West of a diversity of symbolic universes, some partial, some more holistic, and a number overtly dismissive of the West's Christian legacy.

The Enlightenment
Giving inspiration, legitimacy and momentum to many humanistic movements in the post-Reformation period was a radical and holistic symbolic universe, the Enlightenment (late seventeenth to the early nineteenth centuries). This offered the power of belief in the ultimate authority of human reason, progress through rational change and the scientific method, and the centrality of humanistic values, such as liberty and tolerance. It sought the separation of church and state.

---

[14] For how many aspects of daily religious life remained the same post-Reformation, see Duffy, *The Stripping of the Altars*.

Over subsequent centuries, these convictions drove the emergence of numerous other symbolic universes.

Capitalism

As trade and commerce increased across the world from the sixteenth century onwards, the rise of capitalism heralded the creation of a new economic symbolic universe. This emphasized the right to earn and own private property, the centrality of free enterprise, free trade and the fundamental importance of competition. It is a symbolic universe which has increasingly shaped the values and development of every nation and, in more recent years, become a force driving economic globalization. In the twentieth century, the United States became the country most fully embracing this form of symbolic universe, though Russia and China have since incorporated it into their socialistic forms of society (see below).

Colonialism, nationalism and imperialism

The mercantile exploits of European countries set the seal for the age of discovery (sixteenth and seventeenth centuries) and the emergence of colonialism (notably in the nineteenth century). At the same time, the seventeenth century saw growing weariness with wars of religion, especially between Roman Catholic and Protestant nations. The Treaty of Westphalia (1648), in principle at least, confirmed acceptance of national self-determination and the coexistence of sovereign states.

The rise of nationalism, in theory another kind of symbolic universe but very diverse in its expression, fostered movements espousing "the rights of man",[15] with the American War of Independence (1775–83) and the French Revolution (1787–99) being typical. Nationalism heralded the rise of a form of symbolic universe often encapsulated within written constitutions which were used both to affirm communal values (such as "Liberty, Equality and Fraternity") and to shape the growth of democratic government.[16]

---

[15] Thomas Paine, 1791.

[16] Linda Colley, *The Gun, the Ship and the Pen: Warfare, Constitutions, and the Making of the Modern World* (London: Profile Books, 2021).

The nineteenth century witnessed European nationalism merging into full-blown imperialism, initially represented by the conquests of Napoleon after the French Revolution had lost its impact. Exploration of and claims to the "new world" had been underway for some centuries, but the latter part of the nineteenth century saw "the scramble for Africa" giving fresh impetus to the rival imperialistic claims of European nations. The British Empire developed the most global imperial form of symbolic universe, embracing economic, institutional and nationalistic Christian values and norms shaped by the assumption of cultural superiority. Nationalistic claims to colonial territories exacerbated rivalries and fears which eventually sparked the First World War.[17]

Socialism and Marxism

The nineteenth century witnessed the emergence of the economic symbolic universes of socialism and Marxism as alternatives to capitalism, both of which during this period gave impetus to the greater involvement of the working classes in political life. Communism, albeit in nationalistic form, shaped the development of numerous countries, notably the Soviet Union, during the twentieth century. In England, socialism became the driving force of a growing Trades Union Movement and the emergence of the Labour Party, which gained power in parliament for the first time in 1924. Clause IV (not revised until 1994) of its original constitution called for the "common ownership of the means of production, distribution, and exchange, and the best obtainable system of popular administration and control of each industry or service".

The church in England post-Reformation

The most significant prototype of a new Christian symbolic universe to come to the fore during this period was the so-called Puritan Revolution, personified by Oliver Cromwell and embodied in the Commonwealth when, from 1649–60, England and Wales became a republic. Freedom of religious worship was allowed for all except Roman Catholics and Episcopalians. The Anglican episcopacy was ended. More stringent rules

---

[17] Margaret MacMillan, *The War that Ended Peace: How Europe Abandoned Peace for the First World War* (London: Profile Books, 2013).

about public moral conduct were imposed, such as insistence on Sunday observance and limitations of informal social intercourse. However, this form of Christian symbolic universe was short lived with the Restoration of the monarchy in 1660 seeing a return to the old order. From then on, the Church of England moved centre-stage again. However, there was a growing toleration of post-Reformation churches.

Post-Reformation, the church in England gradually lost its former influence in spite of periodic revivals, such as that of Methodism in the mid-eighteenth century and the Oxford Movement of the mid-nineteenth century. However, during the nineteenth century, the Sunday School movement boomed, and churchgoing and the propriety of Christian family life remained relatively stable and undisturbed.

More disturbing for the future of the institutional church was the philosophy of the Enlightenment and prolific scientific, technological and educational advances which gave it momentum. Lesslie Newbigin comments:

> ... the church failed to challenge this new *cultus publicus* effectively and took the road which the early church had refused; it retreated into the private sector. The new vision was allowed to control public life. The 'enlightened' world carried its message, its science and technology, and its masterful relation to the world, into every part of the globe. The Christian vision was allowed to illuminate personal and domestic life, but not to challenge the vision that controlled the public sector. The church took on more and more the shape which the early church had refused: it became a group of societies which were seen as offering spiritual consolation and hope of personal salvation to those who chose to belong.[18]

Newbigin argues that the church's steady retreat into the private world is illustrated by a changing approach to history.[19] The Bible with its vision

---

[18] Lesslie Newbigin, *Your Kingdom Come* (Leeds: John Paul, The Preacher's Press, 1980), p. 29.

[19] Newbigin, *Your Kingdom Come*, pp. 29–30.

of the meaning and end of humankind's universal history was replaced by one derived from the new experience of mastery over nature through science and technology. This divergence of historical perspective led to a protracted ideological debate over the traditional doctrines of the Christian faith and, as a result of Darwin's theory of evolution, about the credibility of major parts of the biblical record. Consequently, world history came to be taught as a humanistic interpretation of the past and present. The Bible continued to be taught but more as offering a range of stories relevant to personal morality and individual behaviour.

Nevertheless, as Tom Holland as well as Catholic Social Teaching argue, the sanctity of human life, the affirmation of human dignity, the equality of human beings and care for the poor and disadvantaged, all of which developed further during this era, had deep Christian foundations.[20] A symbolic case in point was the campaign for the abolition of the slave trade, with Christians and those of other convictions working together, which extended over the first half of the nineteenth century. So too was the ministry of the churches to the poor and destitute in the new urban conurbations of the nineteenth century. Learning for a wider population was furthered through the proliferation of church schools. Thus, beneath the surface of a self-confident Enlightenment which questioned the rational foundations of Christian faith, the legacy of the kingdom community and its gifts, freed from a restrictive Christendom and the constraining mores of a post-Reformation culture, continued to inform and open up "the Western mind".

From the First World War to the present
After a relatively stable century, the slaughter of the First World War, followed by the devastating Spanish flu epidemic, came as a massive culture shock to the West. Old empires, German, Austrian-Hungarian, Ottoman and Russian, collapsed. A long period of economic hardship ensued, with a worldwide financial depression in the early 1930s. Britain and France emerged from the war as "victors", but the consequences of

---

[20] Tom Holland, *Dominion: The Making of the Western Mind* (London: Abacus, 2019) and Anna Rowlands, *Towards a Politics of Communion: Catholic Social Teaching in Dark Times* (London: T&T Clark, 2021).

their failure to respond humanely to the post-war situation of Germany were all too obvious 20 years later. Belief in the unstoppable progress of any kind of rational and humanistic symbolic universe was shattered.

Over the rest of the twentieth century a number of diverse symbolic universes appeared seeking to fill this ideological vacuum. Overall, they remained dominantly secular or humanistic in nature though occupying very different positions running from strongly collective (on both the right and left on the political spectrum), to strongly individualistic (liberal) symbolic universes.

Collective symbolic universes
Collective symbolic universes have often used the veneration of cultural memory, an exclusive ideology and the promotion of nationalistic solidarity to assert their communal identity and primacy in relation to others. Though world trade has remained a gateway to influence, geo-cultural boundaries have been very closely guarded. Leadership, individual or party political, has remained authoritarian and centralized, and the wellbeing of the individual has been subordinated to what is deemed to be the collective good.

Symbolic universes of this kind have emerged on both the "right" and "left" of the political continuum. Examples of the former were the fascist regimes led by Mussolini and Hitler. Examples of the latter have been the USSR of Stalin's era and Mao's China at the time of the Cultural Revolution (both incorporating a Marxist form of political determinism). More recently, these have morphed into the autocratic and centrally controlled "capitalistic" model of Russia[21] and the party controlled "capitalistic" model of China.[22] Over the past decade, this more collectively oriented, nationalistic and culturally, yet autocratically, led and closed type of symbolic universe has become more prevalent in Europe, as in the case of Hungary and Poland, and within the Indian sub-continent.

---

[21] See M. Galeotti, *A Short History of Russia: From the Pagans to Putin* (London: Ebury Press, 2021).

[22] See Kerry Brown, *Xi: A Study in Power* (London: Icon Books, 2022).

Liberal symbolic universes

During the twentieth century, there has also been the emergence of symbolic universes of a so-called liberal disposition, epitomized by "the West". Enlightenment values have remained strong. The focus has been on the individual and on human rights. Societies representing this type of symbolic universe have generally been "democratic" in nature with checks and balances put in place to limit the power of an over-mighty state or individual. However, they too are concerned to sustain the allegiance and cohesion of their citizens, for example by retaining symbols deriving from a venerated past, as in the case of Britain with its royal family and imperial legacy.

North America, Britain and much of Europe and Australasia reflect this form of symbolic universe. Since the middle of the twentieth century, many former European colonies, not least in Africa, have been handed the West's baton of independence and liberal democracy. However, most have struggled to make this form of symbolic universe work well in (still) tribal societies with little historical experience of managing a democratic form of government.

Islamic symbolic universes

A long declining Ottoman Empire finally collapsed after the First World War and, in 1923, a (secular) Republic of Turkey took its place. However, Islam has continued to impinge on the West mainly through the growing independence and strength of Middle Eastern and North African countries, many of which were placed under British and French rule after the First World War. From the 1980s onward, the growth of Islamic terrorism, directed largely towards the West, and furthered by al-Qaeda, the Islamic State and their satellite cells, increased.

As a prototype symbolic universe, John Turner notes that Islam "speaks to abstract concepts such as the *Umma* (the community of believers) and *assabiye* (group feeling) and relies upon the notion of extra rational agency.... The only sources for inquiry and guide to every aspect of social life have already been divinely revealed through the

Hadith and the *Quran*".²³ It espouses "given" principles guiding all levels of relationships. At the same time, like Christianity over the centuries, Turner argues that Islam has cashed out the beliefs and values of its key texts in closed as well as more open ways. In the case of Islam, he calls these "traditional" and "non-traditional" schools of political thought.

"Traditional" Islam

The traditional Islamic school of thought can be regarded as "totalitarian". To some extent it reflects the culture of Christendom. Traditionalists divide the world into two realms, *Dar al Harb* (the realm of war), under the control of Muslim forces, and *Dar al Islam* (the world beyond under the hegemony of infidels—in particular, the West). Traditionalists seek a homogeneous Islamic world and refute the idea of the sovereign nation state.

The Salafi/Jahadi symbolic universe is an even more radical development of the traditionalist stance. It is not so much a reaction against the latter as a utopian worldview arising from the circumstances of the late twentieth and early twenty-first centuries, for example, the failure of Russia and the West in Afghanistan, the repercussions of the invasion of Iraq in 2003 and disillusionment with the Arab Spring in 2010. It encompasses an idealistic model of Islam "infused with an Islamic hyper-realism and universalism that is in stark opposition to the neo-liberal Western order".²⁴ The enforcement of strict Sharia law is seen as the only way to achieve an Islamic symbolic universe and global political order.

"Non-traditional" Islam

Non-traditionalists are a relatively recent addition to Islamic political thinking and are more accommodating to liberal concepts. They recognize that universal Islamic hegemony is impossible and accept some accommodation to the idea of the sovereign nation state. They seek to

---

23 John Turner, "Islam as a theory of international relations?" (2009) at <https://www.e-ir.info/2009/08/03/islam-as-a-theory-of-international-relations/>, accessed 5 May 2023.

24 Ibid.

adapt to Western mores and modernization without allowing it to weaken a more personal sense of Islamic identity.

Internationalism
Alongside these symbolic universes, some more historically embedded than others, that of "internationalism" gradually emerged in the twentieth century with various attempts to institutionalize it. The First World War had shown that the so-called "balance of power", which had dominated international relations for most of the nineteenth century, was insufficient to prevent a major war. The overt response was the founding of the League of Nations in 1920, inspired by the efforts of President Woodrow Wilson, though the United States never became a member. The membership of the League was only 63 countries, and, despite its ideals, it could do nothing to prevent a Second World War. Germany had withdrawn in 1933.

After the Second World War, the League was succeeded by the United Nations whose Charter was signed in 1945, with five permanent members of its Security Council—the United States, the United Kingdom, France, the Soviet Union and the Republic of China. Its Charter allowed for the sovereignty of nations and the right to collective security and defence. This and other projects of the United Nations were committed to increasingly open borders, reliance on international organization for managing relations among states, fewer constraints on global trade, arms control, and the global promotion of democratic government and human rights.[25] The World Bank, to make capital available for investment, and the International Monetary Fund, to facilitate international trade and commerce, were set up following the Bretton Woods Conference in 1944. The result of these post-war developments was a new global network of international organizations and specialized agencies intended to facilitate peace and economic co-operation between nations.

---

[25] P. Vioti, "Nationalism vs. Internationalism: Fears, Uncertainties and Geopolitics in Europe", in R. Belloni et al. (eds), *Fear and Uncertainty in Europe: The Return to Realism?* (Cham: Palgrave Macmillan, 2019), pp. 35–52.

The hopes of the United Nations were set back by the onset of the Cold War between the USSR and the West, resulting in the formation of NATO in 1949 and, the USSR's response, the Warsaw Pact, in 1955. The Berlin wall went up in 1961. For three decades afterwards, the West experienced the threat of a nuclear-armed USSR, and the consequences of China's Cultural Revolution (1966–76), bringing fear of communist domination in numerous parts of the world, notably Vietnam where the United States engaged in a prolonged war from 1955 to 1975.

At the same time, European countries were seeking more open relationships and freer trade arrangements, beginning with the creation of a six-nation European Coal and Steel community in 1952. This and other economic treaties eventually led to the setting up of the European Economic Community in 1957, with the United Kingdom joining in 1973, and the emergence of the European Community in 1993 as an economic and monetary union.

The Cold War came to an end in 1989 with the USSR integrating *Glasnost* (openness) and *Perestroika* (restructuring the economy and politics) into its system. The USSR broke up in 1992. By the turn of the millennium, Russia was moving towards an oligarchic form of capitalism and autocratic leadership. Meanwhile China's economic "miracle" was underway driven by a rejuvenated Chinese Communist Party.

The economic management of a global economy was to the fore in meetings of the G7 group of nations, initiated in 1975, the G20 meetings inaugurated in 1999 and in the World Economic Forum of business leaders and politicians, set up in 1971, and now meeting annually in Davos. In 2020, the theme for the G20 was, significantly, "stakeholders for a cohesive and sustainable world".

These diverse expressions of "Internationalism" introduced glimpses of a new symbolic universe onto the world scene. Its principles remained dominantly Western, in many ways reflecting its Christian legacy but rarely explicitly acknowledged as such. Although that universe underpinned much of the work of the United Nations, a number of countries, notably those espousing communist or Islamic ideals, continued to call this legacy into question. Within this symbolic universe, as Max Weber argued, emerged a symbolic sub-universe of an economic nature built on capitalistic principles which, as globalization increased, greatly enhanced the wealth of humankind but exacerbated the inequalities between rich and poor countries.[26]

This "brave new world", which in the 1990s was deemed by Francis Fukuyama to represent "the end of history",[27] was to receive a profound culture shock from the 9/11 attack on the twin towers in New York, the global financial collapse of 2008 and "the Arab Spring" (2010) and its violent repercussions. Since then, it has been Russia's seizure of the Crimea in 2014 and invasion of Ukraine in 2022, the explosion of the migrant crisis in 2016, the "Make America Great Again" presidency of Donald Trump in the USA (2017-21), the disarray of the European Union after the Brexit referendum (2016), the Covid-19 pandemic and, most ominous of all, the growing climate change crisis, which together have demonstrated the limitations of internationalism as a symbolic universe able to resolve the communal dilemma and create a sustainable and flourishing global community.

The church after the First World War

The church in Western Europe during this time experienced a gradual loss of credibility, especially after the First World War. That war engendered disillusionment with the Victorian project, with all its optimism, relative peace and economic and industrial expansion. The war also led to perplexity as to what the church, and the symbolic universe it represented, could do to save humanity from itself.

The Second World War accelerated a lack of confidence in the church to address the needs of the age. It was an attitude which drove the 1960s generation, and those that followed, to reject the church as an anachronistic institution out of touch with the changing mores of the era; racial, youth, feminist and sexual.

Clericalism remained entrenched throughout this period. A charismatic revival in the 1980s and 1990s, and evangelical revival from

---

[26] Max Weber, *The Protestant Ethic and the Spirit of Capitalism* (Oxford: Oxford University Press, 2010 [1905]). See also R. H. Tawney, *Religion and the Rise of Capitalism* (West Drayton: Pelican, 1948 [1926]).

[27] Francis Fukuyama, *The End of History and the Last Man* (London: Penguin, 1992).

the 1990s onwards, did little in the West to stem the downward spiral. Only the emergence of new black and independent evangelical churches witnessed numerical growth, but their membership remained relatively small.

However, despite this numerical decline, two happenings offering some hope of resolving the communal dilemma were the ecumenical movement, which I consider in more detail later, and the Second Vatican Council. A worldwide ecumenical movement was initiated by a World Missionary Conference held in Edinburgh in 1910. This led to a number of themes of Christian and public concern, such as "life and work", being addressed by the churches during the inter-war years. The first assembly of the World Council of Churches was held in Amsterdam in 1948. It is now a fellowship of 350 member churches spanning over 110 countries.

Though the Roman Catholic Church has never formally joined it, dialogue has continued. The ecumenical movement was given a massive boost by the Second Vatican Council (1962–5) convened by Pope John XXIII. This also inaugurated swingeing changes in the Roman Catholic Church, such as permitting the liturgy in the vernacular and the affirmation of the laity as "the people of God".

A British Council of Churches was set up by William Temple in 1942. This grew in influence and diversity over the century, embracing all the mainstream churches except the Roman Catholics. It was renamed Churches Together in Britain and Ireland in 1990. However, the ecumenical movement in the UK lost a good deal of momentum over the second half of the twentieth century.

The communal dilemma—an unfinished agenda

If the term to sum up the form of symbolic universe which appeared in the West prior to the Reformation is "homogeneous", that for the post-Reformation period would be "heterogeneous". Europe, existing in an ever-expanding world, remained at the forefront of many transformative discoveries and developments. At the same time, disillusionment with a restrictive Christendom and warring of "Christian" churches and nations after the Reformation led to a vacuum filled by the emergence of a range of competing secular symbolic universes.

Nevertheless, the post-Reformation era saw many of the gifts of the kingdom community continuing to be embedded in Western society, as witnessed in the development of civic law and legal constitutions.[28] For example, exemplifying the gift of liberation, society gradually came to accept, in principle at least, the dignity of the individual and the equality of humankind, the end of the slave trade and child labour, in the nineteenth century, and the growing status of women, during the twentieth century, being illustrative. The physical and mental health of human beings, key attributes of the gift of life, and the importance of education for all, intrinsic to the gift of learning, came to the fore during the latter part of this period. In the UK, the creation of the Welfare State after the Second World War was illustrative of the gift of love.

Internationalism grew apace. It was driven forward by the economic and technological advances of the period, making the vision of a diversity of nations coming together to build a global community of communities seem not quite so utopian. In this quest, a growing number of intermediary agencies, from the UN (secular) to the World Council of Churches (religious), played an important role.

However, despite these advances, the communal dilemma, the problem that every social collective faces when the wellbeing of humankind requires that it becomes and remains open to others without undermining its own strength as a community, remained what at times seems to be the default condition of humankind. It was typified by the two most recent world wars and later the more limited but hugely destructive conflicts in the Balkans, Middle East and, most recently, Ukraine. It produced the Cold War across the second half of the twentieth century, as well as the rise of militant forms of Islam in the early twenty-first century.

---

[28] See Colley, *The Gun, the Ship and the Pen*.

6

A Christian symbolic universe for the twenty-first century

The Christian legacy revisited

I contend in this book that one reason why the communal dilemma is so hard to resolve is that neither sacred nor secular world orders have understood, or have been willing to accept, the global communal promise of the symbolic Christian universe revealed in the life and teaching of Christ. It is my conviction that this symbolic universe, incarnate in the kingdom community and its gifts, which is at the heart of Christianity's legacy to the West, holds the key to the surmounting of the communal dilemma and the creation of a global community of communities. In this sense, a Christian symbolic universe is not just one more contribution to a theory of international relations, it provides a "theory" of international relations in its own right. That it may claim to be divinely inspired does not make it invalid. The test of its validity is whether or not it works.

I have outlined the main features of a Christian symbolic universe and the kingdom community which embodies that universe at the outset of this book. Here, before exploring how in practice that universe might transform society and lead to the creation of a global community of communities, I need to look in greater depth at two key features of that universe. First, I consider the unique nature of that universe's legitimation. Secondly, I explore why the communal dilemma can only be surmounted if the gifts of the kingdom community (life, liberation, love and learning) build on, integrate and make universal the core components of the sociology of community (a sense of security, significance, solidarity and socialization).

Christian symbolic universe	An authoritarian symbolic universe
Type of authority	
Trinitarian	Human
Christ as the symbolic person	Those in power as symbolic persons
Servant leadership	Directive leadership
Communal—collective	Unilateral—autocratic/oligarchic
Default attitude—human nature as fundamentally altruistic	Default attitude—human nature as fundamentally self-seeking
Nature of power	
Trinitarian gifts	Human self-sufficiency
Primacy of love	Primacy of fear
"Maternal"—redemptive	"Paternal"—judgemental
Chosen—liberating	Imposed—controlling
Empowerment	Subjection
How exercised	
Shared power—human and divine	Reliance on the "balance of (human) power"
Covenant—trust	Contract—law
Openness—inclusion	Closure or domination—exclusion
Co-operation—partnership	Competition—rivalry
Education	Indoctrination

Legitimation

To explore that which legitimizes and gives authority to a Christian symbolic universe, I set out some of its key features alongside its polar opposite, an authoritarian and closed symbolic universe. Several forms of an authoritarian symbolic universe, both "right" and "left" wing, appeared in the twentieth century. Over past decades, similar kinds of authoritarian legitimization have appeared in countries such as China, Russia and Iran and, more recently, in Hungary, Sweden, Italy and Israel.

Authoritarian symbolic universes, if allowed to dominate the global scene, would destroy all hope of surmounting the communal dilemma and of creating a global community of communities. What I present in the chart above are two "ideal-types". In practice, there will be numerous exceptions to the characteristics I list. However, I hope this approach will enable some of the major features of these two forms of symbolic universe to become clearer.

Type of authority
The most significant feature of a Christian symbolic universe is that it takes the Trinity to be its ultimate authority and source of its power. Trinitarian authority is symbolized by the figure of Christ and the nature of the authority, servant leadership, which he exercised, embodying the roles of visionary, strategist, catalyst, intermediary, enabler, educator and partner.

The authority of the Trinity as an entity emphasizes that a Christian symbolic universe is founded on a communal form of authority. It is the authority of a divine collective not of an all-powerful individual or group. This accords with our conviction that the only form of internationalism which can ultimately survive and flourish will need to be essentially communal; a sovereign and a people in partnership, engaged together in kingdom community building within society and world.

A Christian type of legitimating authority assumes "the glory of man" and that to be fully human is to realize and affirm the divine potential within everyone.[1] An authoritarian authority normatively assumes and plans to control the negative consequences of human nature.

The nature of power
The power given to humankind by the Trinity is conveyed by the gifts embodied in the kingdom community: life, liberation, love and learning. These can be set over against those with which humankind is naturally endowed and on which it attempts to rely. Each divine gift matters in the building of a universal and inclusive kingdom community, though the greatest is that of love. An authoritarian symbolic universe exercises

---

[1] David Jenkins, *The Glory of Man* (London: SCM Press, 1966).

control though the promotion of the fear of authority. Power within a sacred symbolic universe has a "maternal" quality, with forgiving and redemptive attitudes underpinning it. In an authoritarian context, a "paternal" form of power, judgemental and sometimes punitive in character, is normative.

How power is exercised

The legitimating authority and power of the Trinity is employed to enable human collectives to be transformed by the gifts of the kingdom community. Its stance of servant leadership invites humankind to be "a full and equal partner" in that task. Its approach to relationships, be they personal, national or international, is not about creating a "balance of (human) power" in the hope that this will protect individuals or collectives from harm.[2] It is about demonstrating that the way to tackle the communal dilemma is to further security and trust through partnership, human and divine.

The Trinity exercises power on the basis of a profound mutuality between itself and the kingdom community. It is a covenant relationship. Authoritarian leadership relies on law, a formal contract often imposed from above, to maintain control.

The Trinity demonstrates that a key aspect of servant leadership is to foster the work of every collective committed to enabling human collectives to live together with and learn from one another in the building of one world. Such servant leadership often involves exercising the role of intermediary or go-between in order to surmount the communal dilemma by facilitating the building of bridges and the crossing of boundaries. Authoritarian symbolic universes are exclusive and competitive, not least playing on the threat, real or imagined, of other individuals or collectives in order to maintain control.[3]

The Christian symbolic universe seeks to employ the kingdom community's gift of learning, with all its attributes, to educate its members. The authoritarian symbolic universe turns to indoctrination as a means of retaining its power.

---

[2] An important feature of the theory of "internationalism".

[3] This underlay the assumed threat to the UK of the European Union and the arguments for Brexit.

A way forward?
A common reaction to the proposition that a Christian symbolic universe, and the Trinitarian legitimation on which it rests, offer a means of addressing the crises we now face has been to deride it as based on naïve faith not clear reason and, therefore, utopian and beyond the capability of humankind.

There is no doubt that commitment to such a universe is an act of trust and hope. But so, ultimately, is commitment to all theories of human relationships, from the interpersonal to the international. It should be remembered that this Christian "theory" of international relations is based on the record of the life and death of a human being who practised the gospel of the kingdom which he preached. His message was profoundly counter-cultural at that time. Yet many of its principles and values have been slowly absorbed into and enriched the Western way of life we know today. It is an institutionalization process which, at times, has been very slow. It has also been costly for its advocates and all those who have sought to raise the stakes of what it means to be fully human.

Nor, as already argued, have any secular symbolic universes hitherto proved any better at solving the communal dilemma. At best, they have achieved a temporary and insecure cessation of hostilities. Any communally sustainable way forward which they may at times have seemed to offer has relied ultimately on their drawing on the gifts of the kingdom community and incorporating the legacy of a Christian symbolic universe.

The gifts of the kingdom community—value-added, universal and complementary

The gifts of the kingdom community, life, liberation, love and learning, together with servant leadership, exemplify the power of a sovereign Trinity made communally meaningful and available to humankind and embodied in a Christian symbolic universe. They are explicit and experiential gifts of grace which make that universe far more than a utopian concept.

These gifts have a number of fundamental qualities or virtues which enable them to contribute to building communities which are strong, open and inclusive, essential attributes for resolving the communal dilemma. First, as communally transformative gifts, they add communal value and depth to the most that the basic *sociological* components of community (a sense of security, significance and solidarity, socialization and social control) have to offer. This is of fundamental importance because community as feeling (its sociological foundation) has time and again been exploited to create closed collectives, sacred and secular, all too often set over against one another (what I have called earlier "the dark side of community").

I have already noted in brief what I believe to be some of the main attributes of the gifts of the kingdom community. In revisiting this Christian legacy, I look in more detail below as to how those gifts and their attributes add value to the primary sociological components underpinning them. This remains an in-depth and ongoing journey of discovery. I here summarize a number of what I see as significant contributions, past and current, to that quest by way of introducing the reader to the deeper meaning of the gifts of the kingdom community.

Life transforms security

Some sociologists, such as Zygmunt Bauman, regard (physical and material) security as the basic building block of community. He is right that "security is a necessary condition of dialogue between cultures".[4] Theories of international relations that are built on human insecurity, and which regard fear of others as necessary to keep the peace, can never suffice. Walls, however high, cannot for ever protect a collective. To overcome fear of "the other" by withdrawal into the ghetto, or by seeking to dominate those feared, is a recipe for disaster. Russia's attempt to secure its borders against an imagined aggressor, NATO, by trying to force neutrality on Ukraine, is a case in point.

Achieving a sense of security, though communally imperative, is never enough to tackle the communal dilemma. A sense of security has

---

[4] Z. Bauman, *Community: Seeking Safety in an Insecure World* (Cambridge: Polity Press, 2001), p. 142.

to be freed from the survival-instinct or the quest for supremacy so that it can embrace the gift of life's other attributes such as health, vitality, creativity and care of the planet. It is only such attributes of the gifts of life which can bring a sense of the richness of life, and potentially of all relationships, and end an inhibiting preoccupation with "them" over against "us".

Pope Francis (2015), Laudato Si'

Some idea of the "value-added" nature of the attributes of the gift of life can be gathered from Pope Francis' encyclical letter *Laudato Si'* subtitled "On care for our common home".[5] In this profound reflection on humankind's relation to the natural environment Pope Francis argues that "care of the planet" is about far more than concern for nature as "a system which can be studied, understood and controlled". It necessitates a response to creation "understood as a gift from the outstretched hand of the Father of all, and as a reality illuminated by the love which calls us together into universal communion".[6]

That response is first and foremost one of wonder and awe which evokes "praise to God" for "our common home" which, as Francis of Assisi put it, "is like a sister with whom we share our life and a beautiful mother who opens her arms to embrace us".[7] However, "we are (also) called to be instruments of God our Father, so that our planet might be what he desired when he created it and correspond with his plan for peace, beauty and fullness".[8]

This does not mean an attempt by humankind to dominate nature driven by "a technological paradigm" allowing "the method and aims of science to shape the lives of individuals and societies".[9] This has led to the dire situation in which we now find ourselves with "the earth, our home

---

[5] Pope Francis, *Laudato Si': On care for our common home* (London: Catholic Truth Society, 2015).
[6] Pope Francis, *Laudato Si'*, p. 40.
[7] Pope Francis, *Laudato Si'*, p. 7.
[8] Pope Francis, *Laudato Si'*, p. 29.
[9] Pope Francis, *Laudato Si'*, p. 55.

... beginning to look more and more like an immense pile of filth".[10] It means realizing that we are one with the whole of creation for "everything is connected".[11] As a human family, including the poor and marginalized, we are called to "work together in building our common home".[12] "There can be no renewal of our relationship with nature without a renewal of humanity itself."[13] Thus the resolving of our divisions (the communal dilemma) becomes imperative.

For this to happen, a Christian paradigm (symbolic universe) needs to be embraced which enables humankind "to recover the values and the great goals swept away by our unrestrained delusions of grandeur".[14] It is a Trinitarian paradigm legitimated by "the Father (as) the ultimate source of everything, Christ, his reflection, (as the one) through whom all things were created" and "the Spirit, infinite bond of love (as) intimately present at the very heart of the universe, inspiring and bringing new pathways".[15]

There remain a multitude of challenges ahead and issues to be resolved which are far from clear cut. What, for example, are the implications of life as a divine gift for personal concerns such as abortion, same sex relationships and assisted dying? On a societal level, what should be our response to the unruly growth and pollution of cities, water poverty, exploitation of the earth by multinationals, the "deification" of the market[16] and national ambivalence in addressing the massive implications of climate change? Pope Francis' response is that a global Christian paradigm makes it clear that these matters can only be resolved by humility in recognizing our place in God's creation, human dignity being accorded to all, the quest for "a new and universal solidarity"[17] and a readiness to contribute to and learn from open dialogue with those

---

[10] Pope Francis, *Laudato Si'*, p. 16.
[11] Pope Francis, *Laudato Si'*, p. 47.
[12] Pope Francis, *Laudato Si'*, p. 12.
[13] Pope Francis, *Laudato Si'*, p. 60.
[14] Pope Francis, *Laudato Si'*, p. 58.
[15] Pope Francis, *Laudato Si'*, p. 112.
[16] Pope Francis, *Laudato Si'*, p. 31.
[17] Pope Francis, *Laudato Si'*, p. 13.

sharing this planet with us. Such a response necessitates us drawing on the other core gifts of the kingdom community.

Liberation transforms significance

To have a role to play in family, neighbourhood or society is communally essential for both individuals and collectives. The communal dilemma cannot be resolved if it leaves any participant without a sense of self-worth. However, a sense of significance founded only on the affirmation of others can be a fickle sentiment. For example, remove any person from a public role and its recognition and their sense of significance will be much reduced.

For anyone to experience the greatest, most sustainable and fulfilling sense of significance, an experience of the unmerited but unshakeable divine dignity bestowed on every person is imperative. "Even the hairs of our head are numbered" (Luke 12:7). Christ taught us that not even a sparrow falls to the ground without God noticing, and that we are more valuable than many sparrows (Matthew 10:29–31). Despite the immense diversity of human beings, Christian faith is founded on the affirmation that all matter and each counts, above all the weak and marginalized. From this follows the equality of every human being in the sight of Trinity.

However, a Christian symbolic universe recognizes the fallibility of human nature and how it blocks the way to the recognition of what it means to be fully human. That universe offers the gift of liberation, which transforms the attribute of significance, as part of a redemptive and renewal process available to the whole of humankind. Such liberation enables human beings to be released from captivity to self, to realize what it is to be truly human and to experience a profound sense of their divine worth. What is true for individuals is true for collectives. Whether or not they are communally strong or weak, recognition of their limitations and openness to the gift of liberation can pave the way for recognition of their divine worth.

Larry Siedentop (2014), Inventing of the Individual: The Origins of Western Liberalism

I have identified some of the key attributes of liberation as—significance, human dignity, equality, justice—redemptive and distributive, forgiveness and reconciliation. However, the concept of human liberation, or freedom, has more to it than any single list of attributes can encompass. I here look at the contribution of Larry Siedentop and Graham Tomlin to an understanding of the gift of liberation.

Siedentop describes how in Greek and Roman times there was the assumption of natural inequality. In all aspects of daily life, there was an acceptance of a social hierarchy, with males dominating the scene and slaves at the bottom of the scale. The family, the tribe and the city or state took precedence over the individual. It was the apostle Paul who sowed the seeds of a revolution in three respects. First, that God had overturned the Jewish view that obedience to the law gave a person status in the eyes of God. Second, that Christ's death on the cross, normally the lot of slaves, had upended the accepted social hierarchy of the day (1 Corinthians 1:18–25). Third, that in Christ, ethnic, social and gender distinctions carried no weight in relation to how God the Father viewed his children (Galatians 3:28). Thus Paul's "conception of the Christ laid the foundation for a new type of society".[18] It was one in which Christian liberty meant accepting the premises of moral equality and reciprocity, of "equal liberty".[19] It was a freedom not to indulge "the flesh" but to love and serve one another. Such freedom was symbolized by the sacrament of baptism which "stood for liberation from the confusions of paganism as well as the literalism of Judaism".[20]

This revolutionary thinking took many centuries to be understood, accepted and implemented. A fundamental issue at stake was what sort of legitimation was required to give authenticity and sovereign authority to a slowly emerging Christian symbolic universe and what did this say about the status of the diversity of members of the institutions and society which

---

[18] Larry Siedentop, *Inventing the Individual: The Origins of Western Liberalism* (London: Allen Lane, 2014), p. 63.

[19] Siedentop, *Inventing the Individual*, p. 77.

[20] Siedentop, *Inventing the Individual*, p. 71.

constituted that universe. Siedentop traces the history of this tension in the history of the West over subsequent years. It was prevalent in the life of the monastic movement from Benedict onwards, though there was much here, such as the validation of human labour and care of the poor, which affirmed the human dignity of all. Throughout Christendom pope and emperor continued to vie for ultimate legitimation in a highly structured feudal society which was built on serfdom. On a local basis, it was the priesthood which monitored and guided how people interpreted their place in the divine order of things.

Nevertheless, Siedentop argues, within Christendom deference to those in authority and ongoing gender distinctions mattered less than the gradual "translation of moral equality into the primary social role".[21] A distinctively Christian legal system based on canon law developed which was grounded "on the equality of souls in the eyes of God".[22] It linked together the concepts of personal choice and personal responsibility, thus opening up the concept of justice. Even though the church abrogated the right to determine how this worked out in practice, retaining its ultimate authority as given, it was a principle which "could, one day, be turned against the church as well as secular rulers".[23] So it proved. In fact, "the proto-liberal beliefs which had developed within the church by the fifteenth century—the belief in moral equality and a range of natural rights (based on natural law), in a representative form of government and the importance of freer enquiry—only came together when they were deployed against the church's claim to have a right to 'enforce' belief, with the help of secular rulers".[24]

It was mounting opposition to that claim, witnessed in particular in the Reformation which put an end to confessional unity and led to the birth of modern liberalism, that brought about the separation of church and state and the emergence of "secularism".[25] Siedentop believes that it was not the Renaissance but Christianity which was the root of

---

[21] Siedentop, *Inventing the Individual*, p. 122.
[22] Siedentop, *Inventing the Individual*, p. 213.
[23] Siedentop, *Inventing the Individual*, p. 213.
[24] Siedentop, *Inventing the Individual*, p. 313.
[25] Siedentop, *Inventing the Individual*, p. 333.

"the conviction that uncoerced belief provides the true foundation for 'legitimate' authority".[26] It was on that foundation that the West came to uphold the freedom of the individual and "the privileging of equality—of a premis that excludes permanent inequalities of status and ascriptions of authoritative opinion to any person or group—which underpins the secular state and the idea of fundamental or 'natural' rights ... Christianity played a decisive part in this".[27]

Siedentop's conclusion is that the emergence of the "secular", of the autonomy of the individual and the "equal liberty" of all human beings, is not a threat to Christian faith but a profound outcome of it. Indeed, "Secularism is Christianity's gift to the world, ideas and practices which have often been turned against 'excesses' of the Christian church itself".[28] "The atmosphere of the New Testament is one of exhilarating detachment from the unthinking constraints of inherited social roles. Hence Paul's frequent reference to 'Christian liberty' ... The deep individualism of Christianity was simply the reverse side of its universalism."[29]

However, two major threats remain to the West's Christian heritage in this connection. "The first is the temptation to reduce liberalism to the endorsement of market economics."[30] The other is "individualism", the retreat into the private sphere of family and friends at the expense of civic spirit and political participation.

Graham Tomlin (2017), Bound to be Free: The Paradox of Freedom

Graham Tomlin pursues a similar quest for the meaning of human liberation. He describes how "the invention of the individual", as Siedentop argues, given impetus by Christianity, led to an ongoing search for how human dignity and freedom of choice could be furthered in Western society. The intention was for individuals to be liberated from the inhibiting nature of laws, traditions and customs enforced by a

---

[26] Siedentop, *Inventing the Individual*, p. 335.
[27] Siedentop, *Inventing the Individual*, p. 63.
[28] Siedentop, *Inventing the Individual*, p. 360.
[29] Siedentop, *Inventing the Individual*, pp. 353–4.
[30] Siedentop, *Inventing the Individual*, p. 363.

conservative and dominating authority, be that imperial, royal, feudal or ecclesiastical.

This libertarian movement gained impetus from the sixteenth century onwards. Protestantism encouraged the individual to face God alone, whilst its ethic encouraged the rise of capitalism and drove the individual to stand economically on their own feet. Over subsequent centuries, political scientists like Thomas Hobbes, John Locke, Jean-Jacques Rousseau and John Stuart Mill set out ways in which the values, forms and governance of societies might be radically reshaped to ensure the autonomy of the individual.

Tomlin traces how the libertarian movement merged into the human rights movement of the twentieth century. The latter was in large part a response to the inhumanity of the treatment of Jews by Germany during the Second World War. It was given overt expression in 1948 by the UN Declaration of Human Rights and numerous similar declarations that followed it.[31] However, Tomlin argues that the human rights movement remained peripheral until the 1970s, when the focus of interest shifted from the self-determination of groups and nations to the rights of the individual.

"The libertarian vision of freedom assumes the autonomous individual as the basic unit of social life."[32] However, in its classical or modern forms, many questions can be asked of it. Who defines the meaning of autonomy and the rights which are presumed to accompany it? Should the focus be on the individual, as in the West, or on groups such as the family and tribe, as in certain Eastern cultures? How is it decided which freedoms are paramount and which secondary? How can the search for autonomy be built into a political programme? What authority guarantees that the latter is achieved and maintained? Behind all these questions lies the foundational matter of "what it means to be human".[33] Not least, the Achilles heel of autonomy, how do we handle the brokenness of human beings and the dark side of human nature?

---

[31] Graham Tomlin, *Bound to be Free: The Paradox of Freedom* (London: Bloomsbury, 2017), p. 186.

[32] Tomlin, *Bound to be Free*, p. 198.

[33] Tomlin, *Bound to be Free*, p. 187.

Furthermore, insistence on the autonomy of the individual can lead to the creation of "an adversarial culture",[34] which obliges an appeal to some external authority to protect human rights. The outcome can be either anarchy, if this fails to materialize, or the alternative of autocracy and submission to "the surveillance state",[35] a situation which has been repeated time and again throughout history.

A Christian symbolic universe and liberation: Over against the libertarian vision of freedom, Tomlin sets that which springs from the values and norms of a Christian symbolic universe, embodied in what I have described as the kingdom community. This accepts that human beings need to be liberated from "the state of nature" or, as Paul puts it, from bondage to destructive elemental powers which have resulted in "our fallen state" (Romans 8:18–23; Galatians 4:3). In the case of the Gentiles, Paul probably had in mind forces represented by pagan gods. In the case of the Jews, he focused on the oppressive and divisive influence of a "divine" law and its "ethnic boundary markers such as circumcision"[36] which resulted in Judaism treating other cultures as inferior. Paul's vision was of "a new community which disregarded divisions in social status, and so could experience freedom from social competitiveness, or the usual ethnic divisions in Greco-Roman society".[37]

How was this to be achieved? Unlike the libertarian or human rights view of freedom which turns inwards and envisions the individual as a blank slate, the Christian pathway to liberation is to turn away from preoccupation with personal autonomy and freedom of choice and allow oneself to be grasped by the majesty, beauty and compassion of a loving God, "a perfect community of Love—the Trinitarian God of Christian faith".[38] We are not called to imitate God but to be in relationship with him. That relationship is made possible by "the faith of Christ" (Galatians

---

[34] Tomlin, *Bound to be Free*, p. 184.
[35] Tomlin, *Bound to be Free*, p. 63.
[36] Tomlin, *Bound to be Free*, p. 103.
[37] Tomlin, *Bound to be Free*, p. 190.
[38] Tomlin, *Bound to be Free*, p. 204.

2:16),[39] who through his life, death and resurrection enabled human beings to be set free from slavery to self and adopted as children of the Father. It is a relationship which is "not a right but a gift".[40]

However, liberation in Christian terms is not only about freedom *from* self-centredness and self-sufficiency, it is *for* the task of creating community. Tomlin writes:

> Freedom is found, paradoxically, in the glad and welcome acceptance of the other as a gift, not a threat; individuality which serves not to isolate us from one another or from God, but which instead creates relationship. It is found in a view of human life as essentially communal before it is individual; that sees us constituted first and foremost by our relationships, not our separateness.[41]

At the heart of that relationship is a new law, the Great Commandment. "You shall love your neighbour as yourself" (Galatians 5:14), and its corollary to "bear one another's burdens and so fulfil the law of Christ" (Galatians 6:2). The authority exercised by the Trinity is empowering and, when accepted, transformational. The Book of Common Prayer describes this transformational experience as entering into a relationship with a God "whose service is perfect freedom". As Simone Weil argues, such "freedom (is) a skill to be learnt, not an assumption to be made. It is a kind of adaptability whereby the mind masters the body to accomplish the tasks which need to be done to make a community function well".[42] It is a discipline which requires "attention" not just to goodness and beauty but to God as a Person. "Freedom therefore comes not in an act or through the exercise of personal will ... but from looking in the right direction."[43] Here we see, as with all the gifts of the kingdom

---

[39] Tomlin argues that this is just as legitimate a translation of this verse as "through faith in Jesus Christ".
[40] Tomlin, *Bound to be Free*, p. 108.
[41] Tomlin, *Bound to be Free*, p. 202.
[42] Tomlin, *Bound to be Free*, p. 82.
[43] Tomlin, *Bound to be Free*, p. 85.

community, that none exists in isolation from the rest—in this case the gift of liberation overlaps with the gifts of love and learning.

Tomlin concludes:

> The Christian vision of freedom offers something the libertarian or human rights visions do not. Those versions have their merits, establishing freedom from oppression and asserting the right of individuals to certain basic elements to life. What they cannot do ... is to create community. What is needed is a vision of freedom that not only establishes freedom from oppression, but also a foundation for the kind of community life that stretches across the boundaries of ethnicity, class and other divisions that separate people. This can only be found in the idea of freedom as a gift and not a right.[44]

Love transforms solidarity

There are many pleas, sacred and secular, today for a greater sense of solidarity to heal national divisions and overcome the communal dilemma. "Solidarity" is one of the key concepts of Roman Catholic Social Teaching and is put forward as a foundational concept for the social and economic wellbeing of humankind.[45] In his book *How the West Was Lost*, Ben Ryan argues that a renewed sense of solidarity is, alongside liberty and equality, essential for the restoration of Western civilization.[46] However, important as a sense of solidarity is, unless transformed by the gift of love, and enhanced by that gift's other attributes of compassion, empathy, caring and sharing, it remains a potentially circumscribed and tribal sentiment.

To experience the solidarity of the primary group is crucial as part of the quest for community. George Simpson, many years ago, put the issue as follows: "The challenge facing humankind ... is the problem

---

[44] Tomlin, *Bound to be Free*, p. 195.
[45] For example, *Compendium of the Social Doctrine of the Roman Catholic Church* (English edition: London: Continuum, 2005).
[46] Ben Ryan, *How the West Was Lost: The Decline of a Myth and the Search for New Stories* (London: Hurst & Company, 2019), pp. 241ff.

of carrying over the ideal of the primary or face-to-face group ... to the larger group, and ultimately to nations and international action".[47] However, it is my contention that such a "carrying over" requires a power far greater than a sense of solidarity. It can only be achieved by the Trinitarian gift of love, and those attributes—compassion, empathy, caring, sharing and generosity—that enrich it.

C. S. Lewis (1963), *The Four Loves*

The importance of this classic analysis of "the four loves" is that it seeks to deepen our understanding of the gift of love. Lewis argues that only one of his four categories, that of Charity (or *Agape*), has the power to transform the other "natural loves" with that which gives them their divine qualities and prevents their "dark side" from dominating.

Lewis identifies three "natural loves": Affection, Friendship and Eros, and one divine love, Charity. The first three loves have two aspects—that of "gift-love" (such as "that which moves a man to work and plan and save for the future well-being of his family") and "need-love" (such as "that which sends a lonely or frightened child to its mother's arms").[48] Charity, because of its divine origins, consists only of gift-love. The first three loves are constantly merging into one another. However, Charity has an independent and unique role in infusing our natural loves with a divine quality. It is what I mean when I talk about the kingdom community's gift of love.

Affection is the humblest of loves. It has few airs. It is essentially a private love.[49] "Affection obviously requires kinship or at least proximities which never depended on our own choice", states Lewis.[50] "Without Affection (*Storge*) none of us would have been reared."[51] It rubs along with a wide range of familiar people, some not very attractive. It does not expect or demand a great deal. It is not discriminating in its

---

[47] George Simpson, *Conflict and Community: A Study in Social Theory* (New York: Liberal Press, 1937), p. 39.
[48] C. S. Lewis, *The Four Loves* (London: Fontana Books, 1963), p. 7.
[49] Lewis, *The Four Loves*, p. 35.
[50] Lewis, *The Four Loves*, p. 83.
[51] Lewis, *The Four Loves*, p. 56.

relationships.[52] Affection, like all natural loves, can be ambivalent and can work for good or ill. It can become sentimental, possessive (parents craving the affection of older children) or jealous.

Lewis believes love as Friendship is more neglected than in the past, the *Philia* of Aristotle or *Amicitia* of Cicero. It is a love which sees people being "side-by-side" or "shoulder to shoulder".[53] It is often experienced by two people but can extend to a group of colleagues. It is founded on common interests, be these religious, academic or recreational. Friends are often seekers after the same God, truth or beauty.[54] Friendships ignore the physical body. They are freely chosen, co-operative and mutually supportive. They witness people standing "together in an immense solitude".[55] Lewis sees Friendship as "the most spiritual of loves".[56] However, friends are consequently in danger of taking on an air of "corporate superiority"[57] and assuming they have "ascended above the rest of mankind".[58] It is a love on which authority "frowns"[59] as being a potential threat to conformity and one whose intensity and loyalty is not easy to control or tame.

Eros, for Lewis, is simply "being in love".[60] Lewis makes a clear distinction between Eros and Venus, the latter being the explicitly sexual aspect of the former. "Sexuality (Venus) may operate without Eros or as part of Eros."[61] "Sexual desire, without Eros, wants *it*, the *thing in itself*; Eros wants the Beloved."[62] Eros is a preoccupation with one other person. Its seriousness is balanced by play, fun and levity. Eros is the most mortal of loves. Consequently, it is prone to promise what it cannot deliver. It is

---

[52] Lewis, *The Four Loves*, p. 37.
[53] Lewis, *The Four Loves*, pp. 58 and 67.
[54] Lewis, *The Four Loves*, p. 64.
[55] Lewis, *The Four Loves*, p. 62.
[56] Lewis, *The Four Loves*, p. 81.
[57] Lewis, *The Four Loves*, p. 78.
[58] Lewis, *The Four Loves*, p. 83.
[59] Lewis, *The Four Loves*, p. 75.
[60] Lewis, *The Four Loves*, p, 85.
[61] Lewis, *The Four Loves*, p. 85.
[62] Lewis, *The Four Loves*, p. 87.

fickle and needs to be ruled. "The god dies or becomes a demon unless he obeys God."[63]

Lewis believes that these natural loves need to be suffused and disciplined by Charity or they may become rivals to the love of God. "In this yoke lies their true freedom; they 'are taller when they bow.'"[64] Left to themselves, natural loves are never self-sufficient; they eventually vanish or become demons. Charity, divine love, does not supplant natural loves, it transforms them.[65] It summons them to ascend to and thus become diverse expressions of Charity. Charity is wholly gift-love and bestowed by grace. It reveals our need of and total dependence on God (1 John 4:10), one who is "at home in 'the land of the Trinity' (but) Sovereign of a far greater realm". Charity reveals that all human beings are intrinsically loveable and thereby enables us to love one another. Charity can work in those who do not acknowledge God as well as those who do.

Pope Francis (2020), *Fratelli tutti: On fraternity and social friendship*

This is a wide-ranging papal encyclical in which Pope Francis spells out the implications of what he calls "fraternity and social friendship" for the world of today. Whereas C. S. Lewis' concern is in large part the nature of love as experienced by the individual person, Pope Francis' overview is about what the gift of love means in the context of the future of human civilization. He calls us to dream "as a single human family, fellow travelers sharing the same flesh, as children of the same earth which is our common home, each of us bringing the richness of his or her beliefs and convictions, each of us with his or her own voice, brothers and sisters all".[66]

The Pope acknowledges that "solidarity" has become a word that "exists amongst the poor and the suffering and which our civilization ... would prefer in fact to forget ... In certain situations, it has become a

---

[63] Lewis, *The Four Loves*, p. 106.
[64] Lewis, *The Four Loves*, p. 109.
[65] Lewis, *The Four Loves*, p. 122.
[66] Pope Francis, *Fratelli Tutti: On fraternity and social friendship* (Huntington, IN: OSV, 2020), p. 13.

dirty word, a word that dare not be said."[67] Yet "Solidarity, understood in its most profound meaning, is a way of making history, and this is what popular movements are doing".[68] Even so, the Pope prefers to use the term "fraternal love ..., its universal scope, its openness to every man and woman".[69] That love's ultimate source is "the very life of the triune God..., the community of the three divine Persons ... the origin and perfect model of all life in society".[70] Fraternal love is a term taken from Francis of Assisi who interpreted it as an experience which "transcends the barriers of geography and distance, and declares blessed all those who love their brother".[71]

Pope Francis believes that humankind has an urgent need for fraternal love because we live in a world where "the sense of belonging is fading, and the dream of working together for justice and peace seems an outdated utopia".[72] He argues that fraternal love makes possible an advance towards "a civilization of love". "Charity (a synonym for fraternal love), with its impulse to universality, is capable of building a new world."[73] Even so, "Goodness, together with love, justice and solidarity, are not achieved once and for all; they have to be realized each day".[74]

Among the many challenges facing humankind which Pope Francis addresses are neglect of the less able and marginal, the unequal practice of human rights, continuing forms of slavery, war and terrorism, many affronts to human dignity and the creation of "a culture of walls".[75] Pope Francis engages in a passionate appeal for "an open world". He believes our world needs "a new network of international relations".[76] Mutual assistance between individuals or small groups is now not enough.

---

[67] Pope Francis, *Fratelli Tutti*, p. 70.
[68] Pope Francis, *Fratelli Tutti*, p. 71.
[69] Pope Francis, *Fratelli Tutti*, p. 12.
[70] Pope Francis, *Fratelli Tutti*, p. 54.
[71] Pope Francis, *Fratelli Tutti*, p. 9.
[72] Pope Francis, *Fratelli Tutti*, p. 25.
[73] Pope Francis, *Fratelli Tutti*, p. 106.
[74] Pope Francis, *Fratelli Tutti*, p. 16.
[75] Pope Francis, *Fratelli Tutti*, p. 24.
[76] Pope Francis, *Fratelli Tutti*, p. 75.

Practical steps need to be taken, especially in response to those who are fleeing grave humanitarian crises. These include increasing and simplifying the granting of visas; adopting programmes of individual and community sponsorship; opening humanitarian corridors; equitable access to the justice system; freedom of movement and the possibility of employment; ensuring minors' regular access to education; and promoting integration into society.

The Pope argues that there is an innate tension between globalization and localization. However, universal fraternity and social friendship are two inseparable and equally vital poles in every society. "Love for one's neighbour (is) the first indispensable step toward attaining a healthy universal integration."[77] There is a need for greater interdisciplinary communication. Open dialogue is crucial to a new culture of encounter able to overcome our differences and divisions. Forgiveness opens the way to reconciliation; "revenge resolves nothing".[78]

Pope Francis believes that the church is called "to be a sign of unity ... to build bridges, to break down walls, to sow seeds of reconciliation". He ends the encyclical by recalling his meeting with the Grand Imam Ahmad Al-Tayyeb and the appeal they made together for peace, justice and fraternity, "in the name of God, who has created all human beings equal in rights, duties and dignity, and has called them to live together as brothers and sisters, to fill the earth and make known the values of goodness, love and peace ... ".[79]

Learning transforms socialization

By all accounts and definitions, socialization is about the transmission of culture. It is essential for inducting the young, or the incomer, into a way of life that is defined by the symbolic universe shaping the society concerned. However, it offers no guarantees that the latter exists for the wellbeing of cultures other than its own. Socialization may seek to enable

---

[77] Pope Francis, *Fratelli Tutti*, p. 89. Pope Francis has a chapter on the parable of the Good Samaritan at pp. 39–55.
[78] Pope Francis, *Fratelli Tutti*, p. 143.
[79] Pope Francis, *Fratelli Tutti*, p. 161.

the socialized to appreciate and be open to those of a different class or race. However, there is no guarantee of this.

The transformation of socialization into that which can affirm and embrace the riches of other cultures depends on its scope being deepened and widened by the kingdom community's gift of learning and its attributes—a quest for truth, attention, openness, questioning assumptions and person-centred learning. John Hull identifies what he believes to be key components of the gift of learning.

John Hull (1975), School Worship: An Obituary
John Hull describes five models of learning—indoctrination, nurture, instruction, training and what he calls "learning as education". The last is that which is closest to what I have identified as the gift of learning. Each model offers a different understanding of learning's purpose, focus, morality, rationality and the learning process.

Indoctrination is in a category of it own. It is built on a closed understanding of learning. It aims to condition learners in order to recruit them for a particular cause, or to bind them into the culture of a particular collective. It is "immoral", in the sense that its values are imposed, and irrational, in the sense that bona fide evidence is ignored or distorted. Its methods are to imprint the information imparted on the mind of the learner in a way that brooks no questioning and allows no choice. Indoctrination is a learning model typical of those collectives that have become, on the one hand, totalitarian states, or, on the other, closed sects and ghettos. For Hull, there is no way that such collectives can be regarded as learning communities.

Nurture, instruction and *training* share many features in common. All are important as learning processes. The purpose of nurture is to socialize new members of a collective into the culture of that collective. Instruction is about the imparting of basic knowledge. Training is about imparting essential skills. Nurture, instruction and training are "non-moral" in that they take the values of the society concerned as read. They are non-rational in that they take evidence as given. However, in contrast to indoctrination, nurture, instruction and training are "open" models of learning, but only in the sense that their purpose is to prepare the learner for his or her role within society. They are meant to enhance and not to question that role. Tradition and the syllabus drawn from it dominate the learning process.

What John Hull calls *"learning as education"* is quite different in purpose and process from the other models and nearest to our understanding of the gift of learning. It is about learning to learn.[80] It is about "learning for life". It is also about the quest for truth (in our case for the meaning and nature of community). Learning as education entails a journey of spiritual as well as human discovery. It builds on socialization, but a form of socialization which equips participants to question norms and values and is open to learning from alternative symbolic universes as well as its own. Its essential medium is dialogue. Such learning is more than a human endeavour; it is a Trinitarian gift. As Christ said, "When... the Spirit of truth comes, he will guide you into all the truth..." (John 16:13). The learner is offered signs of the kingdom community.

Servant leadership transforms social control
Earlier in this section, I explored at some length the type of authority and nature of power and its exercise which typify a Christian symbolic universe. At the heart of this is the Trinity and the exemplification of servant leadership in the life and work of Christ embodying the roles of visionary, strategist, catalyst, intermediary, enabler, educator and partner. However, the authority of the Trinity as an entity emphasizes that a Christian symbolic universe is founded on a communal form of authority. One illustration of this is the Rule of St Benedict.

The Rule of St Benedict
"For fifteen hundred years, the Rule of St Benedict has been one of the most influential texts in the culture of Western Europe."[81] In 1964, Pope Pius VI declared Benedict to be the patron saint of Europe.

The traditional dates for St Benedict are AD 480–547, although recent scholarship suggests a generation later. Benedict came from a

---

[80] See David Clark, *Breaking the Mould of Christendom: Kingdom Community, Diaconal Church and the Liberation of the Laity* (Peterborough: Epworth Press, 2005), pp. 32–46.

[81] Rowan Williams, *The Way of St Benedict* (London: Bloomsbury, 2020), p. 3.

noble Tuscan family and later studied in Rome. Disgusted by the city's decadent culture he withdrew into solitude but soon attracted a number of disciples. He eventually established a small monastery on Monte Cassino overlooking the road between Rome and Naples. Making use of extensive resources already in existence he composed his famous Rule.

The monastic life had already been in existence for 200 years by the time of Benedict and was by then widespread in the life of the church. Benedict produced a rule based on what was happening around him and his own monastic experience. It came to be regarded as the wisest monastic rule of his day and permeated the lives of thousands of monks in succeeding generations. The Rule's purpose is to establish and keep on course a society, even if a small one, that is Christ-centred. Benedict sought to balance the spiritual needs of such a society with a clear recognition of the frailties of human nature.

The Rule identifies the Abbot as the head of the community and the monks, and others associated with the monastery, as equal brethren. I here focus on the role of the Abbot as one interesting and enduring model of servant leadership, even if some of the qualities suggested may not be currently in vogue today. After a brief overview I touch on the suggested attributes of the gift of servant leadership set out earlier in this book—visionary, strategist, catalyst, intermediary, enabler, educator and partner.

Benedict's Rule envisages a hierarchical form of authority for his monasteries. The Abbot has total oversight and obedience to his decisions is written into the calling of every monk. He is in control of but may be supported by a prior (administration), a cellarer (wellbeing and health), craftsmen and a doorkeeper. However, the Abbot is no despot.[82] Instead he exercises an authority which shows "the tough attitude of a master, and the loving affection of a father".[83] Benedict also describes the Abbot as "a skilful doctor" who cares for all his people and a Good Shepherd who is concerned for all his sheep.[84] At the end of the Rule, Benedict includes

---

[82] Parry (Abbot) (tr.) and Esther de Waal, *The Rule of Saint Benedict* (Leominster: Gracewing, 1995), p. 50.

[83] Parry, *The Rule of Benedict*, p. 13.

[84] Parry, *The Rule of Benedict*, p. 50.

a list of the Abbot's personal qualities, many of which point the Abbot in the way of moderation: "Let him not be restless or anxious, (and) not over-demanding and obstinate, not a perfectionist or full of suspicion."[85] The Abbot is chosen by the community as a whole and after eight years returns to his previous status.[86]

The Abbot stands in the place of Christ, the epitome of servant leadership.[87] His *vision* for the monastery needs to be that of life lived to the full for every member of the community.[88]

His responsibility is "the salvation of the souls entrusted to him"[89] and, to that end, the creation of "a school of the Lord's service".[90] "The Rule is all about relationships, about one person getting on with another and working with a third and taking orders from a fourth and welcoming the interruptions of a fifth, and praying with them all."[91]

The Rule sees the Abbot as a *strategist*. He is a good listener, at times assembling the whole community to hear their views before making a decision.[92] Much of the Rule sets out ways in which he can find a balance between the contrasting needs of the community—between the tasks which need to be done and the individual capabilities of the monks, firmness and toleration, discipline (even to the point of corporal punishment) and nurture. Ultimately, the power of excommunication can be used, the Abbot getting rid of that which would contaminate the community by using "the surgeon's knife".[93] However, here and in many other instances, the offender is given several chances to start afresh.

---

[85] Parry, *The Rule of Benedict*, p. 104.
[86] K. Dollard, A. Marett-Crosby and (Abbot) T. Wright, *Doing Business with Benedict: The Rule of Saint Benedict and business management: a conversation* (London: Continuum, 2002), p. 68.
[87] Parry, *The Rule of Benedict*, p. 11.
[88] Dollard et al., *Doing Business with Benedict*, p. 33.
[89] Parry, *The Rule of Benedict*, p. 14.
[90] Parry, *The Rule of Benedict*, p. 4.
[91] Dollard et al., *Doing Business with Benedict*, p. 11.
[92] Parry, *The Rule of Benedict*, p. 15.
[93] Parry, *The Rule of Benedict*, p. 51.

The Abbot is instructed to ensure that new entries to the community go through a rigorous period of vetting.

The Abbot is a *catalyst* in that he ensures that the daily routine is upheld, being alert to those that might grow idle at work, a key aspect of the life of the monastery, and prayer. The Rule envisages the monastery as a place where people are stimulated to grow and develop, each affirming and nurturing the potential of the rest.

The Abbot is an *intermediary* reflecting the servant ministry of Christ. "His commands and his teaching should mingle like the leaven of divine justice in the mind of the disciples."[94] In his oversight of the community, he should have no favourites, showing himself "equally loving to all, and maintain discipline impartially according to the merits of each".

The role of *enabler* is ever necessary for the Abbot. Where those in the community have gifts and skills the Rule encourages their use.[95] He should take into account whether the monks are of a strong or weaker nature, young or old, healthy or poorly, of an obedient or defiant character. Once again, a moderate and balanced approach to the diversity of the monastic community is urged.

The Abbot is an *educator* in community as "the school of the Lord". "To apt disciples he must explain the Lord's teaching by word, but to those who are hard of heart or simple of mind he must make clear the divine teaching by his actions."[96] "The Abbot must always remember that at the fearful judgment of God two things will be discussed: his own teaching and the obedience of his disciples."[97]

Finally, the Abbot as servant leader is *partner* in both his formal and informal relationships. I have already noted that he may well have assistant leaders to help him, such as a Prior and Cellarer. He encourages his monks to see the inspiration of God at work in the lives of all who work alongside him. "The whole of the Rule is about relationships, and the core quality of building and maintaining relationships of trust."[98]

---

[94] Parry, *The Rule of Benedict*, p. 11.
[95] Dollard et al., *Doing Business with Benedict*, p. 125.
[96] Parry, *The Rule of Benedict*, p. 12.
[97] Parry, *The Rule of Benedict*, p. 11.
[98] Dollard et al., *Doing Business with Benedict*, pp. 31–3.

Genuine guests and visitors are to be welcomed and the Abbot, alongside other forms of care, "with the whole community..., should wash their feet".[99]

The gifts of the kingdom community are inclusive and universal

The gifts of the kingdom community are inclusive and universal. This means that they are offered to every collective, from the family to the nation, available at all times and in all places. They are gifts which have been there throughout history and on offer to people of all cultures and faiths.

In this book, I have focused on these gifts as the Christian legacy to the West. However, they are also the West's Christian legacy to the world. This could be interpreted as yet another form of cultural imperialism. Undoubtedly this has been the case where European empires have distorted and exploited aspects of a Christian symbolic universe in order to impose their own way of life on that of others. However, the universal significance of the gifts of the kingdom community lies in their ability to end not entrench imperialism.

Every gift matters

Every gift of the kingdom community matters. Consequently, problems are created when only one gift, or one of that gift's attributes, is stressed and championed at the expense of the others. For example, those symbolic universes that champion security, an attribute of *the gift of life*, as the ultimate value can lead to the creation of societies that are captive to their own cultures, inward-looking, and fearful or destructive of others. This leads to a world where everything depends on a fragile "balance of (human) power" which may collapse at any unforeseen moment, which happened before the First World War and other times over the past century.[100]

To prioritize the attribute of significance, individual or collective, an attribute of *the gift of liberation*, can lead to a fragmented society and

---

[99] Parry, *The Rule of Benedict*, p. 83.
[100] Margaret MacMillan, *The War that Ended Peace: How Europe Abandoned Peace for the First World War* (London: Profile Books, 2013).

world. Here, Abraham Maslow's idea of a "hierarchy of social needs", not least with "self-actualization" at the top of the pyramid, is, I believe, communally destructive. With a sense of significance as the dominant communal characteristic of a symbolic universe, meritocracy and competition can come to rule the day. A society where the strong get stronger and the weak get weaker is the inevitable outcome.

It is true that certain outcomes beneficial to humankind can emerge if a sense of significance is the symbolic universe's driving force, not least because it impels human beings to compete against one another for status or wealth. Capitalism is the dominant economic symbolic universe which represents this situation, a universe which has brought great benefits to some but impoverished others. However, that such a universe has to be tamed by so many contrived checks and balances reveals its inherent communal weaknesses. Capitalism may appear to address the communal dilemma in so far as it offers an international economic symbolic universe, but in reality it promotes that dilemma because it sustains a deep divide between the rich and powerful on the one hand, and the poor and weak on the other.

To make solidarity, an attribute of *the gift of love*, the ultimate good can all too often lead to placing the wellbeing of the collective as a whole over against the humanity and self-fulfilment of the part, be that the individual or another collective. The danger here is neglect of the *distinctive* contribution of each part, individual or collective, and a dehumanizing and deskilling homogeneity imposed for the sake of the assumed greater good. Such has been the outcome, on the left, with "communist" universes and, on the right, with authoritarian regimes. Both alternatives perpetuate the communal dilemma.

Unless the kingdom community is recognized as, like the Trinity, a holistic concept founded on the universal and the inclusive gifts of life, liberation, love, learning and servant leadership, and given sustainability by divinely guided and empowered human endeavour, the vision of a global community of communities will not become a reality.

7

The process of communal institutionalization today

In this chapter, I look in more detail at the process of communal institutionalization and offer a wide range of examples of how this might be achieved in practice.

Symbolic figures

One of the ways in which a new symbolic universe and its institutions emerge is through beliefs and values advocated by counter-cultural social movements radically impacting on institutions that uphold an existing symbolic universe. In that process, symbolic figures are important in focusing public attention on the beliefs, values and norms embraced by the embryonic symbolic universe. These help to clarify as well as give personal dynamism to the direction of social and cultural change. As Anna Rowlands, in her review of Catholic Social Teaching, writes: "There is a danger of being seduced by the world of (papal) social encyclicals into abstract high theory and forgetting the power of social movements and charismatic individuals who are able through the power of repetition in a particular moment to use language as a potent force to shape history."[1]

Symbolic persons at the heart of new movements have in the past needed to be free to travel because the communities which they sought to mobilize and network were dominantly communities of place (see

---

[1] Anna Rowlands, *Towards a Politics of Communion: Catholic Social Teaching in Dark Times* (London: T&T Clark, 2021), pp. 67–8.

below). Consequently, such figures as Paul, the founders of many religious orders and John Wesley were symbolic figures inspiring, resourcing and turning a host of small and often isolated communities into a movement for radical social and religious change.

As society has developed many more means of interpersonal communication and rapid travel over the centuries, and especially now in the age of the internet, it has become less and less necessary, though still important in order to offer the dynamic of personal charisma to a movement, for symbolic figures to be always on the move. The emergence of movements for communal change has also been facilitated by the proliferation of communities of practice (see below) over recent centuries which form more because of common interests than the physical proximity of their members.

Groups—communities of place and practice

The type of groups involved in furthering the development of a new symbolic universe will be very varied. However, when addressing the matter of communal transformation, it is important to distinguish between those groups which are *communities of place* and those which are *communities of practice*.[2]

Groups which take the form of *communities of place* are those which come into being *primarily* because their members live in close proximity, though shared interests continue to play a part in bringing people together. Communities of place enhance a sense of security and the physical wellbeing of their members. They may vary considerably in size from small groups to whole streets, neighbourhoods and sometimes larger areas. Those who are members of such communities often have little need, desire or ability to travel very far—young families, those limited by physical or mental disabilities, the retired and the elderly. The strength of communities of place will vary in relation to a range of variables including the clarity of the area's physical boundaries, how many generations have lived there, the presence or absence of symbolic

---

[2] I continue to use the word "group" to embrace both these forms of community.

buildings and other notable physical features, the nature of the area's amenities, such as shops and transport, and the adequacy of its public services.

Groups which take the form of *communities of practice* are collectives drawn together *primarily* by common interests.[3] They have emerged as the means of communication and travel have made human encounter and interaction across physical barriers less and less of a constraint. Etienne Wenger describes communities of practice as groups which gain communal strength through "the sustained pursuit of a shared enterprise".[4] Their membership is made up of those for whom mobility is normative. Communities of practice are normally small-scale but, as in the case of communal organizations, can be a good deal larger if common interests are very strong. They usually endure for some time, but as temporary communities of practice, such as those meeting to address an immediate social or political concern, can be an important springboard for communal change.

This book is particularly concerned with two kinds of communities of practice. The first is those which can go a good way to communalizing established institutions. Wenger has written at length about the importance of such communities of practice in relation to the world of business and commerce, though they are commonplace in every kind of institution from education to government.[5] I call these groups *institutional* communities of practice. The other kind of community of

---

[3] R. M. MacIver and C. H. Page, in *Society: An Introductory Analysis* (London: Macmillan, 1950), pp. 32–3, distinguish between "common" and "like" interests. "Common interests" are those we can only pursue together, such as running a company or playing football. "Like interests" are those we share with others but can pursue privately, such as watching television together or listening to a concert. It is common interests which normally create communally stronger collectives.

[4] E. Wenger, *Communities of Practice: Learning, Meaning and Identity* (Cambridge: Cambridge University Press, 1998), p. 6.

[5] E. Wenger, E. R. McDermott, W. Snyder, *Cultivating Communities of Practice: A Guide to Managing Knowledge* (Boston, MA: Harvard Business School Press, 2002).

practice is one that forms in order to pursue a particular issue or concern independent of any established institution. Such communities may be drawn together by concerns related to human rights, the wellbeing of the poor or homeless, refugees, climate change and so forth. I call these groups *non-institutional* communities of practice.

The non-institutional community of practice is the form of group with the greater potential *to initiate* the coming into being of a new symbolic universe. This is because its members usually have a very strong commitment to social change and the greater freedom to initiate and pursue it. Nevertheless, institutional communities of practice, though always subject to formal institutional constraints, including close monitoring to ensure that established institutional forms and practices are upheld, can also play a significant role in forging new institutional norms and helping, over time, to further communal transformation.

Social movements

Charles Marsh, in documenting the history of Martin Luther King's beloved community, writes that:

> ... the idea of movement ... appears as a synchronicity of a million unpredictable forces forming themselves against a long-endured humiliation. But which suddenly—or perhaps over difficult periods of struggle and longing—creates new spaces of freedom and growth. We are not only talking about Montgomery, Americus, and Jackson but about Barmen, Warsaw, Johannesburg, and Tiananmen Square, indeed about "the world of God breaking through from its self-contained holiness and appearing in secular life", in Barth's words.[6]

---

[6] C. Marsh, *The Beloved Community: How Faith Shapes Social Justice from the Civil Rights Movement to Today* (New York: Basic Books (Perseus), 2005), p. 214.

Anna Rowlands notes that "(Pope) Francis has given a high priority to the role of mass social movements as the 'social poets' who create mechanisms for participation for the politically marginalized and whose structures lead to a creativity of social solutions".[7] A major contribution of social movements to communal transformation is their ability to harness the commitment and dynamism of communal groups through networking. This facilitates "habitualization", the repeated use of similar words and actions, to produce new values, norms and mores which call into question, whilst providing an alternative to, those of the existing symbolic universe and its institutions.

The art of initiating, framing the purpose of, recruitment for, participation in, communication and the maintenance of morale within social movements is not straightforward.[8] Thus relatively few social movements achieve radical communal change of existing institutions. Nevertheless, the ability of social movements, sacred and secular, to help shape new symbolic universes and further the institutionalization process has greatly increased over recent centuries.

From the invention of the Gutenberg printing press, around 1440, to the computer revolution of recent decades, from the inauguration of the horse-driven stagecoach to the jet-driven airplane, from the coming of the telephone to the emergence of radio, television and the mobile phone, technological advances have continued to enhance the reach and influence of symbolic figures, communities of place as well as of practice and social movements. Even minor symbolic figures can now become recognized globally as "influencers" or champions of a new way of life. Such developments have made the transition from symbolic figures and groups to social movements faster and easier. This has, in turn, facilitated quicker shifts of institutional and societal values and norms.

In the West, one consequence has been an upsurge of movements which build on its Christian legacy embodied in the gifts of the kingdom

---

[7] Rowlands, *Towards a Politics of Communion*, pp. 209–10.

[8] See Paul Almeida, *Social Movements: The Structure of Collective Mobilization* (Oakland, CA: University of California Press, 2019); and Donatella della Porta and Mario Diani, *Social Movements: An Introduction*, 3rd edn (Oxford: Wiley Blackwell, 2022).

community. For example, the past half century has seen profound changes in family life, with marriage becoming more a choice than a duty and divorce more straightforward and less stigmatized. Gender identity is recognized as increasingly pluralistic.[9] Same-sex marriage is becoming more accepted. The status of women has steadily increased and their sexual exploitation by men in power is more frequently challenged. Racial equality has moved forward in many contexts. Education and healthcare for all have become normative expectations. Workers' rights have been greatly strengthened. Concern for the hungry and destitute as for the refugee fleeing oppression has grown. The misuse of natural resources and the threat to the planet from climate change have brought about global criticism.

However, many such changes remain partial or superficial and are not yet firmly embedded in the mores and culture of Western society and even less so beyond. Indeed, it could be argued that the past decade has seen a profound threat to Western culture, not least as witnessed in the undermining of democratic values evident in the United States by Donald Trump's "false election" claims, in Europe as a result of the divisiveness of Brexit and as witnessed in the growing strength of authoritarian rulers worldwide. Nationalism and xenophobia are dominant forces on the international scene. Genuine disagreements remain over gender and sexual issues, with many seeing some more recent legislation as a dangerous threat to traditional norms. Some advances are being questioned, as in the case of the recent national net zero carbon commitments and the ending of "the green levy" in response to the rising cost of energy caused by war in Ukraine. The availability of abortion has been greatly restricted by a recent ruling of the United States Supreme Court.

Nevertheless, a wide diversity of symbolic figures, groups and movements continue to appeal to, explicitly or not, and promote the values underpinning the Christian legacy of the West. This bears out the contention that the foundations of a Christian symbolic universe are still

---

[9] See here the impact of a pluralistic age on the first fully digital generation in Roberta Katz et al. (eds), *Gen Z Explained: The Art of Living in a Digital Age* (Chicago: University of Chicago Press, 2021).

in place, even though the task of securing, sustaining and developing that religious heritage remains an ongoing challenge.

Communal institutions

The intended outcome of the institutionalization process engaged in by symbolic figures, groups and movements representing a Christian symbolic universe is the communal transformation of existing institutions. However, that process can also be initiated from *within* as well as from beyond those institutions, as well as organizations which possess many institutional characteristics. It is here that institutional communities of practice have a key role to play.

The process of communal institutionalization from *within* existing institutions is similar to that initiated from *beyond* those institutions. The process often begins with a key (symbolic) figure initiating some form of communal change. Their communal innovations, and associated values, are taken up by groups (notably institutional communities of practice), being incorporated into the institution as a whole and, over time, possibly taken up by other institutions. I illustrate this process below with reference to institutions and organizations which have developed communal practices within the world of work. However, institutions and organizations within many other sectors, as Tom Holland has argued with regards to the Western world, have also incorporated features typical of a Christian symbolic universe.

8

Kingdom community building in practice

In looking at practical examples of the institutionalization of a Christian symbolic universe through kingdom community building in today's world, my focus is on the West and especially the UK. However, where relevant, as in the case of basic ecclesial communities, I sometimes venture further afield.

I first consider a number of communal developments which have been initiated from *within* existing institutions in the world of work. I then look at this process in the context of the city. Finally, I identify a wide range of groups, movements and related organizations which are taking the process of communal institutionalization forward from *beyond* the boundaries of established institutions.

I then offer examples from *within* the church as an institution (the ecumenical movement and the basic ecclesial communities of Latin America) and *beyond* its institutional boundaries (the basic Christian community movement in the UK) which reveal important features of the communal institutionalization process.

The communal transformation of society: communal transformation from *within* established institutions

The world of work

Anna Rowlands notes that Catholic Social Teaching regards work as of paramount importance to human development.[1] She writes that John Paul II believed that "humans are never, in the context of work, mere

---

[1] Anna Rowlands, *Towards a Politics of Communion: Catholic Social Teaching in Dark Times* (London: T&T Clark, 2021), p. 284.

instruments or simply utile". "Work itself ... is never mere utility. It is always the shaping of people, for good or ill, and it is the shaping of a cultural world." The communal transformation of the world of work is essential in the quest for community.

Groups as *institutional* communities of practice can have a significant part to play in the communal transformation of the workplaces within which they are found. I have written a good deal about their potential for communal transformation within the world of work.[2] Here I offer a few examples of communal groups and movements which I believe are enabling work-related institutions to manifest the gifts of the kingdom.

"The trade union movement" in the UK was born of a host of institutional communities of practice coming together to reshape the nature of the working world for the benefit of workers. A spin-off from the medieval guilds, in the early nineteenth century the movement was formed by communities of practice that were part of working institutions (factories, mines, shipyards, etc.) joining together to ensure security of employment and to benefit the welfare of their members. The groups and the movement they created reflected many attributes of the gifts of the kingdom community, not least those associated with life and liberation.

The trade union movement was legalized in 1872. Thereafter, it witnessed a century of growth, the emergence of a political party representing its concerns and achieved many reforms of institutions associated with the world of work. After "the winter of discontent" (1978-9), the membership of the movement, especially those representing manual workers, declined rapidly. By the second decade of the twenty-first century, the trade union movement was half what it was in the 1980s. Nevertheless, it remains an example of a powerful instrument for communal transformation.

More recently, the "Corporate Social Responsibility Movement" (CSRM), representing a diffuse but significant endeavour for communal transformation, came into being. Its origins lie in the 1960s when the terms "social auditing" and "the responsible company" were first mooted. Influential in the movement's development was a concern for the

---

[2] David Clark, *The Kingdom at Work Project: A Communal Approach to Mission in the Workplace* (Peterborough: Upfront Publishing, 2014).

conservation of the planet's resources. A growing number of companies, representing different forms of institutional communities of practice, have taken the CSRM to heart. These include Ben & Jerry's (ice cream) in the United States and the Body Shop (cosmetics) in the UK which shaped their working culture accordingly. Despite criticism that CSR is a vague and unenforceable concept, the movement has continued as a catalytic force prompting work-related agencies to be more concerned with the welfare of society and their ecological responsibility. It has also encouraged many organizations to draw up ethical codes of conduct. These range from self-generated initiatives to the UN's Global Contract, launched in 1999, with its ten principles focusing on human rights, good labour relations and conservation of the environment.

Over recent years, the world of work as a whole has become increasingly aware of its need to uphold human values reflecting the gifts of the kingdom community. For example, the "Institute of Business Ethics" (IBE) established in 1986, is committed "to champion the highest standards of ethical behaviour in business".[3] It states that any code of business ethics must cover employees, customer relations, shareholders or other providers of finance, suppliers and the welfare of society as a whole. IBE is particularly concerned to encourage companies to draw up their own code of business ethics.

"Business in the Community" is a British business-community outreach charity, founded in 1986, promoting "responsible business" and now having over 600 member organizations.[4] Its declared aims are "to develop a skilled and inclusive workforce, ensure ways of working are good for everyone, deliver a just transition to the climate crisis and regenerate the planet, and help build thriving communities". For many years, it has majored on encouraging companies to free their employees to play an active part in promoting the wellbeing of their neighbourhoods, particularly as communities of place.

"Common Purpose" is a British charity, founded in 1989, which now organizes leadership training programmes around the world, many characterized by aspects of servant leadership. Its purpose is to develop

---

[3] <https://www.ibe.org.uk/>, accessed 9 May 2023.
[4] <https://www.bitc.org.uk/>, accessed 9 May 2023.

leaders who can "cross boundaries"—geographical, generational and with regards to specializations, cultures and beliefs—in the workplace and wider society. Its programmes seek to introduce potential leaders to situations and experiences, sometimes involving disadvantaged members of society, which they would not normally encounter and to test out leadership skills in that context. As of 2019, 85,000 leaders worldwide had taken part in Common Purpose programmes. Common Purpose also works with universities to run programmes for students to develop global leadership skills. They have run free leadership programmes for 18–25-year-olds in the USA, Singapore, Pakistan, Bangladesh, Nigeria, Germany and the UK.

"Economy for the Common Good—UK" (ECG) is a network set up in 2017 as part of a wider movement which began in Austria in 2010.[5] The latter advocates an alternative economic model founded on the principle of "the common good" and co-operation instead of on profit and competition. By the end of 2013, the movement had over 1,400 companies signed up, most on the European mainland. It espouses a number of fundamental ethical values reflecting the gifts of the kingdom community—human dignity, co-operation and social justice, environmental sustainability, transparency and democratic co-determination. It seeks to work with five main stakeholder groups—owners/investors, employees, suppliers, customers and society at large. ECG is fundamentally a grassroots community-based movement. Local chapters, as ECG calls them, akin to institutional communities of practice, are its building blocks.

"The good workplace" and "employee wellbeing" are now commonplace concepts in the working world. There is a wide range of awards given for organizations which meet this communal ideal, although at times such awards can encourage a competitive market culture. For example, "Great Place to Work" has been engaged in this field for 40 years.[6] It describes its mission as wanting "everyone to have the chance to enjoy going to work; to have pride in what they do and who they work for; to enjoy working with their colleagues in an environment

---

[5] <https://www.ecogood.org/>, accessed 9 May 2023.

[6] <https://www.greatplacetowork.co.uk/>, accessed 9 May 2023.

where they feel trusted and valued, and where they are encouraged to develop personally and professionally". It is a mission which encourages institutional communities of practice and the companies which espouse them to manifest the gifts of the kingdom community.

The city—the Human City Institute (HCI)

The West's Christian heritage permeates not only the worlds of business and commerce, but the worlds of established institutions associated with education,[7] health and welfare, law and order, government, and so forth. At the same time, communities of practice associated with these institutions offer the promise of communally enriching the life of the city. I describe below a project, in which I was involved between 1994 and 2000, which illustrates the potential of communities of practice for furthering the communal regeneration of the city of Birmingham.

The mission statement of the Human City Institute was "to enable those who share a vision of Birmingham as a human city to work together with others to make that vision a reality".[8] It was launched as the Human City Initiative in 1994 to encourage Birmingham, a city in the West Midlands, of well over a million people, that was at that time feeling the constraints of a Thatcher government which had little interest in the communal dimension of urban regeneration. Its aim was to be a partner with the public, private and voluntary sectors working together to end what was inhuman about life and work in the city of Birmingham and enable it to become an impressive example of a human city.[9] It was and remains a story of the kingdom community at work in an urban context.

The Human City Initiative was formally launched early in 1995 at a gathering of some 200 people attended by the Lord Mayor of Birmingham. The Initiative's first phase lasted from 1995 to 1997. During these years, as the Human City Initiative, it was an explicitly Christian undertaking,

---

[7] For the communal transformation of the school see David Clark, *Schools as Learning Communities: Transforming Education* (London: Cassell, 1996).

[8] David Clark, *Building the Human City: The Origins and Future Potential of the Human City Institute (1995–2002)* (2011). Available at <https://humancityinstitute.wordpress.com/reports/>, accessed 9 May 2023.

[9] See Appendix 2 for "Twelve signs of a human city" drawn up by HCI.

with a small "core group" of lay people providing most of the personnel and resources to take it forward. A *Human City Bulletin* first appeared in September 1995 and, in time, reached a circulation of nearly 4,000. Such was the momentum of the project that, in 1997, the Human City Institute (HCI) was formed and became a registered charity. It was made up of a governing council, eventually representing nearly 40 Birmingham organizations from the public, voluntary and private sectors, an active group of trustees and a director (myself) with three administrative staff.

Here I focus on two key aspects of the work of the Institute in which communities of practice, linked together by HCI, were to the fore. The first was the "hearings" programme. In the autumn of 1997, HCI mounted a series of ten public "hearings" in the Council House, Birmingham. Their purpose was to bring together a wide range of people from every sector of Birmingham life to share their visions for the future of the city. The overall theme of the hearings was "Imagine Birmingham". Ten hearings were held in all. Their topics included—"Imagine a human education system", " ... human business world", " ... human health service", " ... human police force", " ... human transport system"—and so on. The hearings were attended by some 500 people. Each hearing became in effect a temporary institutional community of practice setting an agenda for the communal regeneration of the city.

In 2000, HCI instigated a second set of hearings. This time the aim was to encourage people to share their visions on topics that were more directly related to their workplace. Nineteen hearings were held. The topics included—"imagine a human family, ... a human school, ... a human play service, ... a human health centre, ... a human hospital, ... a human college of further education, and ... a human university". Once again vigorous debate meant all the hearings taking the form of temporary institutional communities of practice. In one case, the hearings on the human school led to five schools (primary and secondary) opting to become "human city sites" (see below), holding hearings for groups of their pupils (as institutional communities of practice) and committing themselves to implementing the latter's suggestions for enhancing the life of school as a community.

The other key aspect of the life of the Human City Institute of relevance here was its Human Neighbourhood Project. This was initially focused on Birmingham but soon extended to Swindon and Bradford to test out its effectiveness in other very different cities. The Human Neighbourhood Project involved the creation of "human city sites". A human city site was defined as any local group which believed itself to be making a practical contribution to the creation of a human city, thereby associating with HCI's mission statement. The philosophy behind the concept of human city sites reflected the thinking of Leonie Sandercock, who writes about cities requiring not grand schemes of regeneration but "a thousand tiny empowerments", that is, a host of small endeavours generating the synergy required for communal transformation.[10] Human city sites were a mixture of institutional and non-institutional communities of practice, the latter often overlapping with communities of place.

Any group interested in being designated by the Institute as a human city site was asked to offer "a human agenda", which would be made widely known as a means of inspiring and encouraging others. From my personal perspective as director, these were clear examples of the gifts of the kingdom community in operation. A few examples of agendas offered by human city sites were:

- To increase respect for Hindu elderly people (a Hindu association)
- To explore and share the extraordinary rich culture and history of Yemen with the citizens of Birmingham (A Yemeni centre)
- To pioneer the principle of forgiveness as the norm in the school curriculum (a centre for pupils at risk)
- To give women greater self-confidence through singing (a Sikh women's choir)
- To give policing a more human face (a police Operational Command Unit)
- To develop a Birmingham–Johannesburg community link (a One World group).

In return for a commitment by the sites to work at their agendas, HCI pledged to support and help resource them. The Institute sought to

---

[10] Leonie Sandercock, *Towards Cosmopolis: Planning for Multicultural Cities* (Chichester: John Wiley & Sons, 1998), p. 6.

network its human city sites into a potential movement for the city's communal regeneration.

Despite its innovative endeavours, HCI failed to acquire the necessary funding to pursue its pioneering initiatives after 2004. As a result of its hard-won experience, however, it produced a manifesto setting out "Twelve signs of a human city", many of which reflect the gifts of the kingdom community (see Appendix 2). Since 2004, HCI has continued, in partnership with Birmingham's Trident Housing Association, on a much more limited scale with a focus on undertaking and publishing research, notably in the fields of social housing and the needs of the city's ethnic communities.

The communal transformation of society: communal transformation from *beyond* established institutions

In what follows, I identify a wide cross-section of non-institutional groups and the social movements networking them, all of them ongoing. I also include a number of organizations which I believe still meet the criteria for being non-institutional communities of practice because their primary concern is particular issues or concerns of communal significance.

I give particular attention to explicitly Christian collectives as pioneers and models whilst recognizing that many of their endeavours go hand-in-hand with secular initiatives. The fact that the examples I offer are so eclectic is meant to illustrate the enormous potential, particularly in the era of the internet, of a wide diversity of non-institutional communities of practice and social movements to make manifest the gifts of the kingdom community.

I make no attempt here to evaluate in detail how effective such collectives are in giving practical expression to the gifts of the kingdom community. However, I believe that the ongoing tenacity of most of them bears witness to a Christian legacy which remains extremely influential and a considerable resource for humankind's communal future.

In this section, I associate all groups and movements, Christian or secular, with some "attribute" of each of the gifts of the kingdom community. However, I recognize that, in practice, such collectives are usually empowered by more than one such gift or attribute. Many of the collectives chosen are based in the UK, and are thus representative of Western culture, although their impact in this age of rapid communication may be wider. A few are deliberately chosen to indicate similar developments in the wider world. Encouragingly, the examples I have used are a tiny cross-section of a host of non-institutional communities of practice (alongside a vast number of individual endeavours).

The initiatives taken by the groups identified may already be part of, or may in time become, new social movements. The latter, in turn, may already be or may become catalysts for the communal transformation of mainstream institutions and thus help facilitate the further enrichment and extension of the current Western legacy of a Christian symbolic universe.

In the main text I mark groups (of varying sizes) with a "G". I indicate social movements, which sometimes assume more the shape of networks, with an "M". I also include a number of organizations which are working for the communal transformation of society or world. I mark these with an "O".

Gift of the kingdom community	"Secular"	"Christian"
Life		
Group (G)	Sheffield Women's Aid Hope for the Future, Sheffield	Bar Hill Church Cambridge Arts Group "Green" churches
Movement (M)	Extinction Rebellion	Christian Artists' Network
Organization (O)	Médecins sans Frontières Olympic Games Conference of the Parties (COP–United Nations)	Christian Aid

Gift of the kingdom community	"Secular"	"Christian"
Liberation		
Group	L'Arche Community Alcoholics Anonymous	The Iona Community The Corrymeela Community
Movement	Amnesty International Black Lives Matter	Kairos for Palestine
Organization	Truth And Reconciliation Commission (SA)	Community of the Cross of Nails, Coventry
Love		
Group	Centrepoint	Food banks
Movement	Save the Children	St Vincent de Paul Society
Organization	Age UK	MHA
Learning		
Group	University of the Third Age classes	Society of Friends' meetings
Movement	CAMFED (Campaign for Female Education in Africa)	Student Christian Movement
Organization	Schools of Sanctuary (Cities of Sanctuary)	Oasis Multi Academy Trust Woodbrooke Quaker Study Centre

The gift of life
The attributes of the gift of life, as is the case with every other gift, are built on sociological foundations, in this case, *a sense of security*.[11] A number of collectives treat this attribute as of major concern. A local example is Sheffield Women's Aid (G), which has two refuges that house women and children who need a place of safety in the face of domestic violence.[12]

Among other attributes which typify the gift of life is that of *health*, exemplified here by Médecins sans Frontières (O) and Christian Aid (O). Médecins sans Frontières, or Doctors without Borders, is an international humanitarian non-governmental organization of French origin, founded in 1971.[13] It is best known for its medical care and development projects in conflict zones and in countries affected by endemic diseases. It is now working in 70 countries. Christian Aid is a relief and development agency set up in 1945. It describes its purpose as "to work with local partners and communities to fight injustice, respond to humanitarian emergencies, campaign for change, and help people claim the services and rights they are entitled to". It operates in 29 countries in Africa, Asia, the Middle East, and Latin America and the Caribbean.[14]

Vitality, another attribute of the gift of life, is evident on the world scene in the modern Olympic Games (O), first held in Athens in 1898. It is noteworthy that in 2020 the Olympic Games added the word "together" (the gift of love) to the end of its original motto "Faster, Higher, Stronger...". The attribute of *creativity* is reflected on a smaller scale by the Christian Artists Network (M), which started in the Netherlands in the 1960s and now links some hundred affiliated groups.[15] It has held an annual international seminar since 1981. Its aim is to promote fellowship, unity, understanding and cooperation amongst a diversity of Christian artists. The movement stimulates through national and international

---

[11] In this and subsequent sections, I highlight in italics a number of attributes of the gifts of the kingdom community.
[12] <https://sheffieldwomensaid.org.uk/>, accessed 9 May 2023.
[13] <https://www.msf.org/>, accessed 9 May 2023.
[14] <https://www.christianaid.org.uk/>, accessed 9 May 2023.
[15] <http://www.christianartists-network.org/>, accessed 9 May 2023.

networks the development of personal skills, experience and character-building, so that the individual artist can develop his or her potential. On the local scene, the Bar Hill Church Cambridge Arts Group (G) is open to anyone interested.[16] It meets regularly to help members develop their artistic skills and share their knowledge and experience.

Care of the planet is a particularly important attribute of the gift of life. There is a rapidly growing number of "green" or "eco" groups associated with local churches, notably in the UK and United States. Typical of one of a multitude of small green initiatives, Hope for the Future, Sheffield (G), set up in 2013 by an Anglican priest, Michael Bayley, is a charity which works to equip communities, groups and individuals across the UK to communicate the urgency of responding to climate change to MPs.[17] Extinction Rebellion (M), founded in 2018, is now a global environmental movement.[18] It employs non-violent civil disobedience to compel government action to avoid dangerous tipping points in global warming, prevent the loss of global biodiversity and avert the risk of social and ecological collapse. At an international level, care for the planet is the core agenda of the (normally) annual United Nations Climate Change Conference of the Parties (O) initiated in 1997.[19] In 2022, COP27 assembled in Egypt and was attended by nearly 200 states and organizations.

The gift of liberation

Of all the kingdom community's gifts, the gift of liberation has the greatest diversity of attributes. *A sense of significance* forms its sociological underpinning. The *human dignity* and *moral equality* of every human being are among its theological attributes. These are exemplified by the work of the Federation of L'Arche Communities (G/O).[20] This initiative was founded by Jean Vanier in Trosly-Breuil, France, in 1964. It now operates across 38 countries worldwide and consists of 156 communities

---

[16] <https://barhillchurch.org.uk/art-group/>, accessed 9 May 2023.
[17] <https://www.hftf.org.uk>, accessed 9 May 2023.
[18] <https://extinctionrebellion.uk/>, accessed 9 May 2023.
[19] <https://ukcop26.org/>, accessed 9 May 2023.
[20] <https://www.larche.org/>, accessed 9 May 2023.

rooted in the Christian faith. The communities thrive on a mutually supportive relationship between those with some form of disability and those who care for them. Alcoholics Anonymous (G/M), originating in the United States in 1935, and seeking to address wide-ranging needs of alcoholics, is another network of non-institutional communities of practice stressing human dignity and equality.[21]

Other theological attributes of the gift of liberation include *justice, forgiveness* and *reconciliation,* of which there are a host of examples. Illustrating these attributes is the Iona Community and its local groups (G/O).[22] This was founded in 1939 by George MacLeod, a Church of Scotland minister. Its first phase was enabling unemployed workers from Govan, Glasgow, to rebuild the abbey on Iona (*distributive justice*). The community's subsequent phases have been to encourage those associated with it to live out the Christian faith in the areas of *restorative justice* and *peace.*

Specifically related to *restorative justice*, Amnesty International (G/M) was founded in London in July 1961 by English barrister Peter Benenson.[23] It is now a global movement of some ten million people, the largest human rights network in the world. It seeks to promote justice and freedom across the globe with especial concern for individuals who are unjustly discriminated against or persecuted. Black Lives Matter (M) has considerable current prominence.[24] It is an international but decentralized movement founded in 2013. Its stated mission is "to eradicate white supremacy and build local power to intervene in violence inflicted on black communities by the state and vigilantes". It was given a considerable boost in 2020 when there was a passionate international response to the murder of George Floyd by a member of the Minneapolis Police. Other collectives exemplifying attributes of the gift of liberation include the Corrymeela Community (G/O), founded in 1965 by Ray Davey, a Presbyterian minister, and committed to reconciliation and

---

[21] <https://www.alcoholics-anonymous.org.uk/>, accessed 9 May 2023.
[22] <https://iona.org.uk>, accessed 9 May 2023.
[23] <https://www.amnesty.org.uk>, accessed 9 May 2023.
[24] <https://blacklivesmatter.com>, accessed 9 May 2023.

peace in Northern Ireland;[25] and Kairos for Palestine (M), a Christian Palestinian movement which advocates the ending of Israeli occupation and seeks a just solution to the conflict there.[26]

However, outstanding in exemplifying three other attributes of the gift of liberation (*justice, forgiveness* and *reconciliation*) are two clearly focused initiatives. In November 1940, Coventry Cathedral was destroyed by German bombs. It was rebuilt and reopened in 1962. Meanwhile, the cathedral staff established an international association called the Community of the Cross of Nails (M/O) to "heal the wounds of history, to learn to live with difference and diversity, and to build a culture of peace".[27] It now consists of over 250 churches and other groups which engage in prayer for peace and acts of reconciliation.

A second definitive initiative is South Africa's Truth and Reconciliation Commission (O).[28] Established in 1996 and running until 2003, with Archbishop Desmond Tutu as its chair, it established a court committed to *restorative justice* following the end of apartheid. It sought to give a public hearing in different venues across the country to perpetrators of human rights abuses as well as their victims, the former being able to request, and often given, an amnesty from prosecution. As its successor, an Institute for Justice and Reconciliation came into being in 2000.

The gift of love

Attributes of the gift of love are underpinned sociologically by *a sense of solidarity*. The attribute of *compassion* is at the heart of this gift and, very encouragingly, could be illustrated by the life and work of scores of collectives. Here I mention just three. The St Vincent de Paul Society (England & Wales) (M) is part of an international Roman Catholic voluntary movement dedicated to tackling poverty in all its forms by

---

[25] <https://www.corrymeela.org>, accessed 9 May 2023.
[26] <https://kairospalestine.ps>, accessed 9 May 2023.
[27] <https://www.coventrycathedral.org.uk/reconciliation/community-of-the-cross-of-nails>, accessed 9 May 2023.
[28] <https://ijrcenter.org/cases-before-national-courts/truth-and-reconciliation-commissions/>, accessed 9 May 2023.

providing practical assistance to those in need.[29] Founded in Britain in 1844, in England and Wales it now has nearly 10,000 members who visit vulnerable or isolated people to offer them friendship and practical support. Its aim is to show compassion which is non-judgemental and respects the dignity of all. Save the Children (M/O) was founded in 1919 in the UK to better the lives of children through education, health care and work opportunities, especially in areas of war and natural disasters.[30] It is now a global movement operating in 120 countries. Centrepoint (G), a charity offering shelter to homeless young people, was set up by an Anglo-Catholic priest, Kenneth Leech, in a Soho church in 1969.[31] It now has several regional centres across the UK.

Integral to the attribute of compassion are *caring* and *sharing*. *Caring* covers an immense range of endeavours. Two examples of those addressing the needs of the elderly are MHA (formerly Methodist Homes for the Aged) (O) and Age UK (O). The former was an endeavour established in 1943, before the coming of the Welfare State, to support older people needing care. MHA now runs 89 care homes, 69 retirement living schemes and 45 community and befriending services supporting more than 18,000 older people across England, Scotland and Wales.[32] It employs 7,000 staff and enjoys the support of over 5,500 volunteers. Age UK (O) is a registered charity, though now with an international reach, launched in 2009.[33] It combined the operations of the previously separate charities Age Concern England and Help the Aged to form the UK's largest charity for older people. Its services include enabling the elderly to access health care, offering information and advice, a diversity of wellbeing programmes and campaigning. It consists of over 100 local Age UK associations.

The attribute of *sharing* is impressively illustrated by the proliferation of food banks over recent years, with the wider public giving regularly from their weekly shopping and in other ways to support these endeavours.

---

[29] <https://www.svp.org.uk/>, accessed 9 May 2023.
[30] <https://www.savethechildren.org.uk/>, accessed 9 May 2023.
[31] <https://centrepoint.org.uk/>, accessed 9 May 2023.
[32] <https://www.mha.org.uk/>, accessed 9 May 2023.
[33] <https://www.ageuk.org.uk>, accessed 9 May 2023.

1,400 come under the oversight of the Trussell Trust (G) operating alongside nearly 2,000 independent food banks.[34] Many hundreds of UK churches are involved. Food banks have given stalwart support to millions of people through the Covid-19 pandemic and continue to do so through the recent energy and cost-of-living crises, though these are proving an unprecedented challenge.

The gift of learning
The kingdom community's gift of learning builds on but transforms the process of *socialization*. In particular, it is about *the quest for community*, discovering what it means to be human and how to live together as one world. Learning of this kind has the attribute of being *person-centred*. It requires a readiness to *question assumptions*. It is also enhanced by the ability to value and give *attention* to the spiritual dimension of life, not least by being able to discern the gifts of the kingdom community.

Amongst Christian churches in the UK, the Society of Friends (Quakers) (G/O) has become noteworthy for its meetings having many of the attributes of open learning communities.[35] The Society's life and work are rooted in the conviction that Quakers are called to a life-long journey of spiritual discovery. Its book of discipline, *Quaker Faith and Practice*, contains personal reflections recorded over many centuries intended to help Quakers discover what it means to live out their faith in daily life.[36] The University of the Third Age (G/O) is an international initiative whose aim is the education and stimulation of those in their "third age" of life.[37] U3A was initiated in France at the Faculty of Social Sciences in Toulouse in 1973 by Pierre Vellas. The academic model is now used in many other countries. CAMFED, Campaign for Female Education in Africa (M/O), is an international non-governmental, non-profit organization, founded in 1993.[38] Its mission is to eradicate poverty

---

[34] <https://www.trusselltrust.org>, accessed 9 May 2023.
[35] <https://www.quaker.org.uk/>, accessed 9 May 2023.
[36] *Quaker Faith and Practice (QFP)*, 5th edn (London: Religious Society of Friends, 2005).
[37] <https://www.u3a.org.uk>, accessed 9 May 2023.
[38] <https://camfed.org/>, accessed 9 May 2023.

in Africa through the education of girls and the empowerment of young women.

The Student Christian Movement (M) was founded in 1889.[39] It is the oldest grassroots student Christian movement in the UK. Its fortunes have varied considerably over the years, but it has recently grown in numbers again. It states that its values remain "inclusiveness, radicalism and an open and challenging approach to the Christian faith".

Reflecting numerous attributes of the gift of learning are Schools of Sanctuary (O).[40] These are primary and secondary schools committed to supporting all those, especially parents and children, seeking sanctuary in the UK, creating a culture of welcome for all within the school and, particularly important, raising awareness of the situation of asylum seekers and refugees. An open culture is encouraged through the school curriculum and other activities such as exhibitions and outings. An example is the Oasis Academy Watermead (O), a School of Sanctuary in Sheffield,[41] and one of the educationally innovative Oasis Community Learning Academies set up, from 2004, by Steve Chalk, a Baptist minister.[42] Schools of Sanctuary are an offshoot of the Cities of Sanctuary movement (M/O), the first of such cities being Sheffield, an initiative taken by Inderjit Bhogal, a Methodist minister, in 2005.

A UK organization which exemplifies the gift of learning is Woodbrooke College (O), the national Quaker Study Centre in Birmingham.[43] It was established by George Cadbury in 1903. It seeks "to support, inform and transform Quakers and others as individuals and communities . . . to nourish spiritual development . . . and encourage work for a peaceful and just world".

Intermediary bodies

There are a number of all-embracing collectives, often associated with more than one gift (or attribute) of the kingdom community. These

---

[39] <https://www.movement.org.uk>, accessed 9 May 2023.
[40] <https://schools.cityofsanctuary.org>, accessed 9 May 2023.
[41] <https://www.oasisacademywatermead.org>, accessed 9 May 2023.
[42] <https://www.oasiscommunitylearning.org>, accessed 9 May 2023.
[43] <https://www.woodbrooke.org.uk/>, accessed 9 May 2023.

have taken upon themselves the task of linking and networking non-institutionalized communities of practice. They have a very important role in helping to surmount the communal dilemma, facilitating partnerships and social movements and furthering the creation of a global community. I call them "intermediary" bodies or agencies.

Caritas Internationalis is inspired by Catholic Social Teaching.[44] It was founded in 1897. It responds to disasters, promotes integral human development and advocates about the causes of poverty and conflict. It works with the poor, vulnerable and excluded, regardless of race or religion. It is organized at local (parish), diocesan, national, regional and international level. National Caritas organizations are autonomous, but they combine as part of the Caritas Internationalis confederation. The latter was created in 1951 with the aim of promoting greater co-ordination, communication and co-operation among its 160 national members in more than 200 countries across the world.

DIAKONIA, the World Federation of Diaconal Associations, was founded in 1947.[45] It seeks to remind "the church of God's call to service, justice, compassion, and peace for creation". It now has some 80 diaconal associations and orders representing many different churches linked to it. It holds international assemblies and has a regional structure to promote the exchange of experiences, reflection and resources related to diaconal ministry amongst member associations.

As a protype global organization, the United Nations, set up in 1945 following the Second World War, and established as a successor to the League of Nations inaugurated in 1920, exemplifies the communal importance of intermediary bodies.[46] In 1948, the United Nations produced a Declaration of Human Rights, a milestone in the attempt to create a global community of diverse nations. As well as human rights, its concerns are peacekeeping and security, economic development, humanitarian assistance and related global issues. It currently embodies over 190 members representing almost all the world's sovereign states.

---

[44] <https://www.caritas.org>, accessed 9 May 2023.
[45] <https://diakonia-world.org>, accessed 9 May 2023.
[46] <https://www.un.org>, accessed 9 May 2023.

The gift of servant leadership

Servant leadership, the final gift of the kingdom community, is an art which requires a great deal of experience and practice.[47] However, because it also draws heavily on the other four Trinitarian gifts, it retains the character of a gift. I have noted that the roles most closely associated with it are those which Christ demonstrated throughout his ministry—of visionary, strategist, catalyst, intermediary, enabler, educator and partner.

Because of the affinity of the gift of servant leadership with the other four gifts, it is not surprising that those offering a glimpse of what servant leadership is all about should be associated with setting up or developing the kind of groups, movements and organizations described above. The symbolic figures indicated below clearly manifest these qualities.

Because no one person has the ability or skills to fulfil all the roles of servant leader, one of the hallmarks of the latter is their ability to build teams and networks which can encompass the roles needed for the endeavour concerned.

Symbolic figures

Anthony Cohen argues that symbolic figures are extremely important in strengthening and sustaining any collective's sense of community. This is the case with most groups, social movements, organizations and intermediary bodies, referred to above, which are committed to the task of communal transformation. Symbolic figures are often associated with more than one of the gifts of the kingdom community. They usually exercise roles associated with servant leadership.

Many symbolic figures are known only by the groups which cohere around them. However, some are associated with communal movements of global significance. Illustrative of the latter, and associated particularly with *the gift of life*, would be such figures as Al Gore and Greta Thunberg. Exemplifying *the gift of liberation* would be figures such as Martin Luther King, Nelson Mandela and, more recently, Volodymyr Zelenskyy. Exemplifying *the gift of love* would be such figures as Mother Teresa

---

[47] For a secular discussion of servant leadership see the debate started by Robert K. Greenleaf, *Servant Leadership* (Valdosta, GA: Greenleaf Centre, 2012 [1970]).

of Calcutta and Desmond Tutu. Symbolic figures reflecting *the gift of learning* are less prominent, but I would suggest such people as Paulo Freire and Michael Sandel. A symbolic figure currently exemplifying many of these gifts would be Pope Francis.

Other symbolic features
It is important to note that also important for engendering a strong sense of community are *symbolic events* like the civil rights march on Washington in 1963, or the release of Nelson Mandela in 1990, and *symbolic places*, such as Lourdes. Communal strength is often enhanced by many symbolic forms of art, music, dance, song and poetry.

The religious orders
I have deliberately omitted identifying above any religious orders as exemplifying the gifts of the kingdom community, in part because their vocations are many and varied and few orders have been founded in recent years. However, most religious orders, as communities of practice, are deeply committed to living out one or more of those gifts. Historically, many religious orders have given impetus to communal movements concerned with such issues as educational reform, care for the poor, social justice, peace-making and care for the planet which have been influential in communally transforming institutional values, not least in relation to the church as such.

As historic symbolic figures representing the religious orders, it might be suggested that St Francis of Assisi exemplifies the gift of life, St Ignatius of Loyola the gift of liberation, many such figures exemplify the gift of love, and St Dominic the gift of learning.

Reflections
The wide cross-section of collectives, both institutional and non-institutional communities of practice, which I have identified above are but a handful of examples indicating some of the ways in which I believe that the gifts of the kingdom community, and their attributes, have been or are being made manifest. Because their purpose is to enhance the communal quality of life not only for those whom they immediately serve but for wider society, I believe that, in one form or another,

such collectives can be seen as diverse manifestations of the kingdom community, whether or not this is recognized by them or others. In this respect, they are heirs of the West's Christian legacy and helping to fulfil the promise of a Christian symbolic universe.

Both the institutional and non-institutional expressions of communities of practice have strengths and weaknesses which need to be acknowledged. *Institutional* communities of practice have the great advantage of being already lodged within organizations or institutions sustaining the existing symbolic universe. This gives institutional communities of practice an assurance of continuity. The institutions within which they operate usually have access to high level decision making, be that local, regional or national. If, therefore, institutional communities of practice manage to persuade the leadership of the institutions in which they are based of the importance of the kingdom community's gifts, they have an opportunity to bring about significant forms of communal transformation.

On the other hand, many **non-institutional** communities of practice have to operate on the margins of society. Consequently, they are more likely to struggle for continuity and stability. The leaders of such communities usually carry limited power and influence in relation to the existing symbolic universe and its governing authorities. The influence of non-institutional communities of practice can, therefore, be more easily checked by established institutions.

On the other hand, non-institutional communities of practice have a passion which is not often found with institutional communities of practice. Small can be not only "beautiful" but inspiring and empowering.[48] Non-institutional communities of practice are also free of normal institutional constraints and can choose the form of any protest targeted at the existing symbolic universe. Their potential for informal networking and their ability to give impetus to social movements for communal transformation is also greater.

The communally creative endeavours of communities of practice are never done. Established institutions are always quick to push back against

---

[48] E. F. Schumacher, *Small Is Beautiful: A Study of Economics as if People Mattered* (London: Blond & Briggs, 1973).

the forces of communal transformation. This is evident in the recent rise of "Trumpism" in the United States where the rallying cry was to "Make America great again", the vote for Brexit in 1916 in the United Kingdom and the war in Ukraine, all examples of the tenacity of the institutional closure and the communal dilemma.

Nevertheless, it needs to be recognized that communities of practice often fail to reflect the kingdom-focused message they seek to exemplify. Groups, movements and organizations, in principle committed to communal transformation, frequently fail to be life-affirming, liberating, loving and learning communities and to demonstrate the qualities of servant leadership. For example, the central staff of Caritas Internationalis needed to be replaced for mismanagement by Pope Francis in 2022.[49] Inclusivity and universality are also sometimes an issue. James Cone, the founder of "black theology" and then a leader of the black power movement in the United States, argued that "God is black" and that "white people must repent of their 'whiteness', becoming 'black' in order to have fellowship with the black God and the oppressed".[50] "Black power" in the United States broke with the ethnic inclusivity of the civil rights movement led by Martin Luther King. It also rejected the black liberation theology of Allan Boesak and Desmond Tutu and the latter's belief in a rainbow nation, in South Africa.[51] Those who have more recently insisted that "black lives matter" need to come to terms with the communal imperative that all lives matter if the communal dilemma is to be surmounted and one world to become a reality.

Those striving for justice and peace can also be at loggerheads with one another, as Gerard Hughes, a Jesuit priest, once noted of certain groups of women protesting in the 1980s against the basing of nuclear weapons at the RAF Greenham Common airbase in Berkshire.[52] Those committed to the liberation of one oppressed group can also forget the

---

[49] <https://www.thetablet.co.uk/news/16150/pope-suspends-caritas-internationalis-leadership>, accessed 9 May 2023.

[50] James H. Cone, *A Black Theology of Liberation* (Philadelphia, PA: Lippincott, 1970), p. 164.

[51] Cone, *A Black Theology of Liberation*, pp. 149–50.

[52] In conversation with myself.

oppression of others. "Black power" gave little attention to the oppression of black women. Even the gift of love can be abused.[53] The mistreatment of children and young people at risk by communities, Christian and otherwise, in the past responsible for their welfare and residential care is a scandal which has only emerged relatively recently.

To surmount the failure of human beings in every form of collective to manifest what it means to be a Christian symbolic universe is a long and agonizing task. Nevertheless, it is in these circumstances that the Trinitarian gifts of the kingdom community, universally offered and embraced by that universe, can demonstrate their transformative and redemptive power.

I have above focused attention on groups, especially communities of practice and social movements, as essential catalysts for the communal transformation of those institutions which do not yet reflect, or fully reflect, the values and legitimation on which a Christian symbolic universe rests. However, I recognize that the gifts of the kingdom community are also made manifest through a myriad of individual interpersonal exchanges.

The communal transformation of the institutional church

There have over recent decades been many Christians involved in groups and movements seeking *the communal transformation of the institutional church* as it exists today, often alongside that of wider society. The same process of institutionalization (symbolic figure(s)—groups—movements—institutional change) is also evident here.

---

[53] See also examples referred to by Rowlands, *Towards a Politics of Communion*, p. 237.

Communal transformation from within the institutional church

I describe below three such movements which emerged from *within* the institutional church. These are, from the late 1950s, the rise of Roman Catholic and Latin American basic ecclesial communities; from 1942, the British ecumenical movement; and from the 1950s in the UK, the movement for lay Christian witness in public life.

Basic ecclesial communities (BECs)

BECs originated in Brazil in the early 1960s, in part inspired by the Second Vatican Council. They were a response by Roman Catholics living in rural areas to extreme poverty exacerbated by the authoritarian nature of that country's political and military leadership. They were also given impetus by a shortage of priests. BECs consisted of lay-led local groups, from some five to 30 in size, meeting once or twice a week to worship, read the Bible and engage in activities to relieve poverty and hardship. Many reflected mini kingdom communities. In the 1960s, they mushroomed, with Brazil having some 70,000 embracing some two and a half million members. In time, BECs spread not only to other countries in Latin America but to Africa and the Far East.

The Conference of Latin American Roman Catholic Bishops was very supportive of this phenomenon in their meetings at Medellin (1968), Puebla (1979) and Aparecida (2007). In the late 1970s and early 1980s, BECs provided the impetus for the development of liberation theology, its chief exponents including Gustavo Gutiérrez (Peruvian), Leonardo Boff (Brazilian) and Jon Sobrino (Spanish). Liberation theology was founded on the conviction that theology should be based on reflective practice (praxis) and that the focus of such practice which mattered above all else was a "preferential option for the poor". Consequently, genuine theology is that which interprets God's purposes for humankind from the point of view of the poor and marginalized. Since this time, concern for other marginalized populations has led to the emergence of theologies such as black theology (the United States), Dalit theology (India) and feminist theology (worldwide).

It was more the emergence of liberation theology than the proliferation of BECs which, in the 1980s, brought a negative response from Pope John Paul II. His stance was not that of opposition to BECs as such. It was that liberation theology was in danger of reifying social structures as "sinful" and, therefore, weakening the church's ministry to individuals who were believed to be alone responsible for sinful acts and whose personal redemption is paramount. Anna Rowlands concludes that "by the end of John Paul II's papacy structural sin remains simply the multiplication or accrual of individual sinful acts into consolidated, calcified structures".[54] At the same time, John Paul II was concerned that liberation theology was too close to a Marxist interpretation of poverty for the comfort of Rome. Since then, Pope Francis has given BECs his blessing without clearly espousing liberation theology and its phenomenological assumptions.

Reflections

In the context of this book, the main point that needs to be made is that, for whatever theological or "political" reasons, the church as an established institution stepped in to prevent BECs becoming a movement with the power to threaten the existing traditional Christian (Roman Catholic) symbolic universe. In this case, it was opposition from the papacy, including admonition from the Vatican's Congregation for the Doctrine of the Faith and the appointment of conservative bishops, which inhibited liberation theology turning BECs into a radical movement for the communal transformation of church and society.

At the same time, it must be acknowledged that BECs themselves were not, as a whole, as radical as a theology of liberation might have depicted them to be. Many were as much religious (the need for spiritual support in the absence of priests) and social (kinship and friendship ties were strong) as political in nature, understandably so when their members were often the poor and disadvantaged. BECs were as much communities of place as of practice, even though social bonding enabled them more easily to confront those forces threatening their physical wellbeing.

---

[54] Rowlands, *Towards a Politics of Communion*, p. 101.

Ecumenism

One movement of paramount importance for communal institutionalization, intended to bring greater unity to the Christian world, is "the ecumenical movement". I give a brief overview of its international development but focus on the British scene.

The springboard for the worldwide ecumenical movement is generally regarded as being the Edinburgh World Missionary Conference of 1910 which gathered mainly Protestant and Anglican delegates together from many churches and nations to affirm their "oneness in Christ". From then on, continuing conferences and councils moved the ecumenical movement forward at a considerable pace both internationally and nationally. Lay leadership, such as that of J. H. Oldham, was prominent throughout.[55]

Notable ecumenical initiatives on the British scene were the 1924 Conference on Politics, Economics and Citizenship (COPEC) and the Oxford Life and Work Conference in 1937. The first gathering was convened by William Temple "to think out the application of Christian principles to the problems of contemporary life". It was an event which paved the way for the coming of the post-Second World War "Welfare State". The Oxford initiative addressed the growing totalitarian threat to Europe, and the churches' shared response to an increasingly secular society.

These and similar gatherings led to the setting up of the British Council of Churches (BCC) in 1942. William Temple, now Archbishop of Canterbury, preached at its inaugural service at St Paul's Cathedral. The BCC was initially made up of 16 member churches and several interdenominational organizations, including the YMCA and Student Christian Movement.

On an international level, talks went on between the two world wars about the founding of a World Council of Churches (WCC). The Second World War prevented its inauguration until 1948. It began with a membership of 147 churches including Orthodox churches but not the Roman Catholic Church. Its first assembly's theme was notably

---

[55] Keith W. Clements, *J. H. Oldham and George Bell: Ecumenical Pioneers* (Minneapolis, MN: Fortress Press, 2022).

"Man's disorder and God's design." Since then, there have been ten more assemblies, their themes echoing the mood of the moment, as with the theme for the 2022 assembly in Germany, "Christ's love moves the world to reconciliation and unity". In 1952, evangelical leaders from 21 countries set up a separate World Evangelical Fellowship.

The WCC currently has 352 member churches who together represent more than half a billion Christians around the world. In 2010, the WCC was instrumental in setting up the Action by Churches Together Alliance (ACT), which "counts more than 140 members in 120 countries, becoming the largest coalition of Protestant and Orthodox faith-based actors working on humanitarian, development and advocacy issues".[56]

The British Council of Churches was closely associated with the WCC. Nationally it worked through local councils of churches, by 1946 there being well over a hundred of these. In 1952, the British ecumenical movement was given impetus by the WCC's Lund Statement: "Should not our churches act together in all matters except those in which deep differences of conviction compel them to act separately?" Nevertheless, despite considerable early ecumenical enthusiasm, practical steps towards greater unity were slow to be taken.

The ecumenical movement was given a considerable boost by the Second Vatican Council. In its decree *Unitatis redintegratio* (The Restoration of Unity) of 1964, it stated that: "The restoration of unity among all Christians is one of the principal concerns of the Second Vatican Council". The decree continued: " ... moved by a desire for the restoration of unity among all the followers of Christ, it wishes to set before all Catholics the ways and means by which they too can respond to this grace and to this divine call". Although for Catholic leaders this ultimately meant a return to the Roman Catholic fold, the decree liberated many lay Catholics to engage with their fellow Christians in local ecumenical initiatives.

In 1964, the BCC's Faith and Order Conference in Nottingham pointed the churches in two important directions. First it recommended the setting up of "Areas of Ecumenical Experiment" to encourage the churches to try out greater local co-operation. In 1973, these were

---

[56] <https://actalliance.org>, accessed 9 May 2023.

renamed as Local Ecumenical Projects, and again in 1995 as Local Ecumenical Partnerships. Second, it called the churches "to covenant together to work and pray for the inauguration of union ... by a date ... (which) ... we dare to hope should not be later than Easter Day 1980".

Talks between the Church of England and Methodists about uniting had begun in 1956, and a report was published on these conversations in 1963. A Unity Commission was set up in 1965 to clarify and refine the proposals. Its report—*Towards Reconciliation*—proposed that the Methodist Church should incorporate the historic episcopate. The proposals passed in the Methodist Conference but failed to get the required endorsement in the Church of England's General Synod. In 1972, the proposals were brought forward again but just failed to get the required majority, that was two-thirds, in the House of Clergy.

In 1972, the formation of the United Reformed Church, bringing together Presbyterians and Congregational churches, was approved. However, a significant number of local Congregational churches opted out of the scheme.

In 1978, a Churches Council for Covenanting produced "Ten Propositions" which were intended to lead to the mutual recognition of ministries and the gradual merging of structures. That the Roman Catholic Church agreed to three of the Propositions gave the local ecumenical endeavours a boost. However, in 1982, the rejection of the Propositions by the Church of England undermined further progress at national level. Yet another attempt to bring the Anglican and Methodist churches together was initiated in 2003 when both churches entered in a covenant for unity. In 2014, both churches committed to specific proposals for unity brought forward by a Joint Implementation Commission. However, since then further objections by factions within the Church of England have continued to shelve any final acceptance of the proposals.

In 1990, the British Council of Churches sought to give more impetus to its ecumenical work by changing its name to Churches Together in Britain and Ireland. It set up regional bodies, such as Churches Together in England, and encouraged local councils to rename themselves accordingly. The growth of Local Ecumenical Partnerships, in many shapes and forms, as well as a great deal of less structured local ecumenical endeavour, has continued though with little hope of further movement nationally.

Over past decades the ecumenical movement has faced a new and challenging dimension. Issues around abortion, the ordination of gay clergy and same-sex marriage have revealed deep rifts not only between churches but within them. The Church of England has been divided in relation to these concerns internationally as well as nationally and Methodism in the UK has seen members leave it because of deep disagreements about such matters.

Reflections

The ecumenical movement of the twentieth century and beyond has been the most significant attempt by the church to overcome the communal dilemma and create a global Christian community since the time of Constantine. However, what has happened on the British scene is symptomatic of the West's response to ecumenism. In other continents, such as Africa, where the need to provide health, welfare and education continues to be more acute, collaboration has gone further.

In Britain, the ecumenical movement has plateaued. At the same time a new ethical cloud on the horizon relating to issues of sexuality and marriage has grown increasingly dominant and led to deep division not only between but within churches. It may be that such divisions will see the ecumenical movement as known since the early twentieth century taking on a quite new dimension, with matters of faith and order taking second place to those of ethical concerns regarding the nature of human relationships.

What the ecumenical movement in the UK has achieved so far is not the communal transformation of existing churches but a greater degree of informal co-operation and partnership between them. However, this has been achieved by Christian institutions that have been unable to break the mould of Christendom, on the one hand, or mend the fragmentation of the church resulting from the Reformation, on the other. As David Hawtin and Roger Paul put it, "In the partnership model the inherent weakness is that very little changes, with the risk that modes of working together remain undeveloped or become blunted by familiar denominational patterns and expectations."[57] Paul Avis sees this impasse in starker terms. Because he agrees with the German Lutheran theologian Wolfhart Pannenberg that, "As the body of Christ the church is the eschatological people of God gathered out of all peoples, and . . . is thus a sign of reconciliation for a future unity of redeemed humanity in the kingdom of God", he believes that "Christian disunity and division is not only an appalling evil in itself but gives birth to even worse evils".[58]

At the heart of the ecumenical movement's inability to achieve its affirmation of "one holy, catholic and apostolic church" has been an inadequate theology of mission. It has become preoccupied with the reconciliation of a divided church rather than the surmounting of the communal dilemma globally and the creation of one world. There has been no communal theology of the kingdom compelling the churches to come closer together and thereby demonstrate to a world in profound crisis how to create a global community of communities. The ecumenical movement has lost its way because it has become more about a church-centred kingdom than a kingdom-centred church.

The churches in Britain remain institutions tied to their past. Those symbolic figures that did emerge to become advocates for the creation of a holistic Christian church seeking to create a holistic world were faced with institutions whose vision of Christian unity did not go further than some kind of ecclesiastical co-operation. The British Council of Churches was a body made up of the representatives of such bodies. As a result, it became an institution built in their image with no power or authority to move its ecumenical endeavours any further than those related to closer forms of partnership. Renaming the BCC "Churches Together" sought after but failed to give any greater impetus to a new way of being church.

---

[57] D. Hawtin and R. Paul, *The Origin and Development of Local Ecumenical Partnerships: Telling the Story* (2011, re-issued 2020) at <https://cte.org.uk/working-together/local/local-ecumenical-partnerships-leps/lep-literature/telling-the-story-the-origin-and-development-of-leps/>, accessed 9 May 2023.

[58] Paul Avis, *Reconciling Theology: Conflict and Convergence in Theology and Church* (London: SCM Press, 2022), pp. 108, 119.

The limited achievements of the ecumenical movement are also the result of it being dominantly a "top down" rather than "bottom up" movement. The latter would require symbolic figures, groups and movements to offer a radically new vision of "one church for one world" which could inspire and drive forward a genuinely ecumenical ("whole world") movement. United endeavours at the local level have sometimes tapped into this radical hope. However, a failure by church leaders to offer an adequate theology and ecclesiology, as well as the passion for a reconciled church, has prevented the emergence of any coherent, strong and sustainable grassroots movement for the communal transformation of existing religious institutions.

Exacerbating the inability of the churches as institutions to move beyond partnership is that they have remained predominantly communities of place. In wider society, not least in the world of work, it is communities of practice which are now the norm, and which hold the key to the communal transformation of society. Because the British churches are dominated by structures geared to engagement with the local scene, they have never developed the ability to engage collectively and effectively with a cosmopolitan and mobile culture. Until this happens, the British churches will remain moulded by institutional structures unable to give impetus to a holistic movement which can exemplify and pave the way towards the communal transformation of the wider world.

The inability of the ecumenical movement on the British scene to move beyond the model of sporadic partnership, as Paul Avis bluntly puts it, leaves "the church . . . unreconciled to itself, to the world and to God, and is therefore barely even the church".[59] I believe that any such "reconciliation" ultimately depends on the church in Britain and elsewhere espousing a communal theology of the kingdom which offers it the vision, incentive and power to surmount the communal dilemma and thereby become a communally holistic church giving impetus to the building of one world.

---

[59] Avis, *Reconciling Theology*, p. xi.

The affirmation of the laity

Another important development on the European scene which had the potential to achieve the communal transformation of the institutional church was the affirmation of the laity. The Reformation had set in motion the liberation of the laity from dependency on the ordained ministry. Consequently, both within the church and beyond people from all social classes began to play a more active role in the church's ministry and mission. I focus mainly on the British scene.

The late eighteenth and nineteenth centuries saw Nonconformist churches in England taking the lead. Many of their members, as within Methodism, were active in the emerging Trades Union Movement, whilst Quakers became entrepreneurs who founded major businesses such as banking and chocolate manufacture. Many lay people moved into politics and became what Alan Gilbert calls "the backbone of British Liberalism".[60] As already noted, laity were active in the ecumenical movement during the first half of the twentieth century, not least in those assemblies convened by William Temple which helped to set the parameters of the Welfare State after the Second World War.

On the Continent, the potential of the laity for driving forward the renewal of church was being mapped out by the French Dominican Yves Congar[61] and the Dutch theologian Hendrik Kraemer.[62] In the 1960s, the Second Vatican Council issued three documents which envisioned the church as "the people of God" in the world.[63] In 1987, the Synod of Roman Catholic Bishops in Rome published *Christifideles laici*, an apostolic exhortation concerning "the vocation and mission of the lay faithful in the church and in the world".

---

[60] Alan D. Gilbert, *Religion and Society in Industrial England: Church, Chapel, and Social Change, 1740–1914* (London: Longman, 1976), p. 181.

[61] Y. M. J. Congar, *Lay People in the Church: A Study for the Theology of the Laity*, tr. D. Attwater (Westminster, MD: Newman Press, 1957).

[62] Hendrik Kraemer, *A Theology of the Laity* (Philadelphia, PA: Westminster Press, 1958).

[63] *Gaudium et spes* (Joy and Hope), *Apostolicam actuositatem* (The Apostolate of the Laity) and *Lumen gentium* (The Light of the Nations).

In the early 1960s, initiatives were taken to establish a European Association of Academies and Laity Centres which, as a key aspect of their programmes, ran consultations and courses on the contribution of the Christian faith to public life.

On the British scene post-Second World War, a number of initiatives were taken to support the ministry of the laity in daily life, notably in the world of work.[64] These included, in 1944, the setting up of the Sheffield Industrial Mission by Bishop Hunter to engage the church more fully in the lives of those working in the steel industry. Also established about this time were two centres for the training of lay people for their ministry in the world of work: in 1947, the William Temple College began its life at Hawarden in Cheshire. It moved to Rugby in 1954. In 1955, Methodism's Luton Industrial College was opened. Both centres were led by influential symbolic figures—the former by Mollie Batten, an ex-civil servant, the latter by William Gowland, a Methodist minister.

A number of other laity centres were also established in Britain. St George's House, Windsor, opened in 1966 to bring leaders from church and society together to discuss issues of public concern. The Roman Catholic Ammerdown Centre was set up in the early 1970s. The vision was for an adult education centre that would translate the aspirations of Vatican II into practice.

The 1960s saw the publication of Mark Gibbs and Ralph Morton's ground-breaking book *God's Frozen People*, in 1964, followed in 1971 by their *God's Lively People*, both titles indicative of their authors' concerns about the role of the laity in public life.

In 1982, John Stott founded the London Institute for Contemporary Christianity in London. In 1987, the Roman Catholic Von Hügel Institute (for the interdisciplinary study of church and society) was established at St Edmund's College, Cambridge. In 1989, the "God on Monday" project (later to become the Ridley Hall Foundation's "Faith in Business" programme) began at Ridley Hall, Cambridge. In 1993, the organization

---

[64] For a more detailed overview see David Clark, *Breaking the Mould of Christendom: Kingdom Community, Diaconal Church and the Liberation of the Laity* (Peterborough: Epworth Press, 2005), pp. 170–87.

MODEM was launched, focusing on developing forms of leadership within church and society informed by Christian faith and values.

From the 1980s onwards, the Church of England set up a number of working parties to explore the role of the laity as the church dispersed in the world. In 1985, it produced a report entitled *All are Called: Towards a Theology of the Laity*, and two years later another, *Called to be Adult Disciples*, both documents relating to the ministry of the laity in society. In 2017, the Church of England produced another report, notably entitled *Setting God's People Free*. This stated that "every one of these (past) reports underscores the same issue: the Church of England must urgently find ways to 'liberate' the laity to become confident disciples in the whole of life. Doing so is an essential foundation for mission and evangelism and a prerequisite for growth."[65] In 1990, the British Methodist Conference approved a report on *The Ministry of the People of God in the World* and recommended it to its members for study.

A number of national conferences focusing on the ministry of the laity were mounted during this period. In 1980, 2,000 people gathered for the Roman Catholic Church's National Pastoral Congress in Liverpool. In 1991, another significant gathering, the Rerum Novarum Conference, was held to celebrate the Pope's encyclical letter of a century before on *The Conditions of Labour*, the first real protest by the Roman Catholic Church at the inhuman conditions experienced by working people during the latter part of the nineteenth century. Also in 1991, the Malvern Conference was held, a major ecumenical event to celebrate the first Malvern Conference 50 years before. In 1999, at the Catholics in Public Life Conference in Liverpool, "for the first time ever, over three hundred Catholics and a sprinkling of invited guests ... came together ... to discuss being a Catholic in public life".

A range of small groups and associations have over the years tried to inspire the institutional church to give more time and support to the ministry of the people of God in the world of work. These include the Industrial Christian Fellowship, the Young Catholic Workers, the Christian Association of Business Executives, the London Institute for

---

[65] *Setting God's People Free* (London: Archbishops' Council, 2017), p. 9.

Contemporary Christianity, the Christians in Public Life Programme,[66] Quakers and Business, and the Kingdom at Work Project.[67] Alongside these have gone a considerable number of evangelical agencies and groups supporting Christians engaged in different occupations.

Reflections

On the British scene, the weakening of the twentieth-century movement which affirmed the laity as the primary resource for Christian engagement with society was clearly evident from the 1970s onwards. It was a retreat symbolized by the closure of the William Temple College in 1971 and of the Luton Industrial College, in 1996.

The number of other laity centres in Britain remained small and their programmes increasingly became more generalized and unrelated to the ministry of lay people in public life.

The reports produced by the Church of England and the Methodist Church had little impact at the local level and were soon gathering dust on the shelves. The national conferences on lay ministry in society were well attended and, at the time, inspired many lay people active in public life. However, there was no follow up and the enthusiasm engendered soon waned.

Most of the dozen or more small associations or groups which were set up at this time to affirm and resource lay witness in society, especially within the world of work, managed to sustain their endeavours but on a very small scale, with little contact between them and very limited impact on the institutional church.

The steady decline of the mainstream churches in the West led to retrenchment and concern for church growth increasingly dominated their missionary agenda. The desire to "make more disciples", not the communal transformation of society, came to be the predominant driver of mission, not least amongst evangelical workplace groups.[68] Even the

---

[66] See Clark, *Breaking the Mould of Christendom*, pp. 174–87.
[67] See David Clark, *The Kingdom at Work Project: A Communal Approach to Mission in the Workplace* (Peterborough: Upfront Publishing, 2014).
[68] See Clark, *Breaking the Mould of Christendom*, pp. 254–64.

concept of "whole-life discipleship",[69] applied to the ministry of the laity by some bodies such as the London Institute of Contemporary Christianity, implied more a discipleship-creating rather than a society-changing ministry. Consequently, the "liberation of the laity" came to mean their orientation towards an individualistic and church growth form of mission rather than one committed to communal transformation.

The clerical profession never lost its dominance as the shapers and, often, agents of mission. This gave impetus to the belief that the only way for the church to engage meaningfully with secular institutions was by means of chaplaincy, a role designed to be one primarily for the ordained ministry and increasingly of a pastoral rather than communally radical kind.[70]

Communal transformation from *beyond* the institutional church

Basic Christian communities

The proliferation of basic Christian communities in the UK was a phenomenon of the late 1960s through to the 1980s which originated more from beyond than within the life of the institutional church.[71] It was triggered by the political and social upheavals of the 1960s, notably evident in the United States as a result of the Vietnam War and the civil rights movement, but also witnessed in the wider radical questioning of existing cultural and sexual norms. These upheavals led to the quest for "an alternative society", which challenged supposedly "authoritarian" institutions including the family, and the emergence of the so-called "communes movement". The latter was mirrored by the setting up of many small Christian communities in the UK and USA.

---

[69] *Setting God's People Free*, p. 25.
[70] For a more detailed discussion of this point see Clark, *The Kingdom at Work Project*, pp. 359–81.
[71] Clark, *Breaking the Mould of Christendom*, pp. 150–87; David Clark, *Yes to Life: In Search of the Kingdom Community* (London: Collins, 1987).

Basic Christian communities were different from the BECs of Latin America. Some were focused on a self-sufficient and communal lifestyle lived out by groups of individuals and families, often in large old houses in rural areas. Others were more issue- or interest-based, their members living together or, more often, dispersed communities of practice. The latter addressed concerns such as justice and peace, environmental and economic issues, how better to care for the poor, serving the homeless or disabled, alternative forms of schooling or new approaches to spirituality.[72] As a whole these groups reflected many of the gifts of the kingdom community. They were usually lay-led and committed to democratic forms of decision-making. Their members were largely middle-class and members of a wide cross-section of churches or none.

In 1981, I was involved in setting up *The National Centre for Christian Communities and Networks (NACCAN)*, based in Birmingham (see Appendix 4). This carried information and news about some 400 basic Christian communities and religious orders in the UK in order to encourage and link their endeavours. The centre produced a regular bulletin and a directory of communities to publicize the work of those involved. During the 1980s, NACCAN convened three national congresses attended by several hundred representatives of the movement.

The number of basic Christian communities went into decline from the 1990s. The National Centre, which by then had moved from Birmingham, closed in 2003. A loose network of communities continued for some years but without the dynamic purpose and scope of the original movement.

Reflections

A number of factors led to the decline of this 30-year initiative. One was the disparate reasons why basic Christian communities originally formed. This meant that they did not possess a common vocation strong enough to create a movement able to address the communal transformation of church or society. It was largely the National Centre, with its bulletin, consultations, congresses and an itinerant director, that

---

[72] David Clark, *Basic Christian Communities: Towards an Alternative Society* (London: SPCK, 1977).

held the communities together. It was also hard for such communities to survive, with finance always a problem, daily work beyond the community concerned scarce, and committed members hard to find to replace those who left.

The National Centre had a large management committee representative of the movement and chaired by the Bishop of Birmingham. Despite this, the mainstream churches, out of ignorance or apathy, took little interest in the movement. Consequently, there was little public awareness of the movement and its potential as a kingdom-centred model of church. Basic Christian communities were regarded as peripheral groups "doing their own thing" on the margins of the institutional church but of little relevance to its mission. Nor did the movement at this stage produce anything akin to a liberation theology which could offer an informed perspective on its potential and sense of direction. As this book indicates, a kingdom theology which could have given the movement sound foundations only emerged much later.

9

A new paradigm—the diaconal church

The state we're in—the church in the UK

The stark reality is that the church in the UK has been in numerical decline for a couple of centuries, even though it is only since the beginning of the new millennium that its long-term survival has become a matter of immediate and pressing concern to its leadership. In the UK, the church has an ageing membership. Baptisms, church marriages and funerals have lost much of their communal power as symbolic public events. The younger generation is increasingly and openly acknowledging a lack of Christian faith and little interest in joining any part of the institutional church.[1] As a pointer to this decline, the 2021 census reported a minority of people in the UK describing themselves as Christians for the first time since records began (46.2 per cent, down from 59.3 per cent in 2011). The ongoing numerical decline is also bringing critical financial problems, made worse by the fact that Covid-19 appears to have further reduced regular church attendance and diminished financial giving.

Meanwhile, the church is landed with the costly upkeep of many historic but crumbling buildings, these often kept going by a handful of an elderly and diminishing membership. This overall decline is matched by a drop in the number of those entering the ordained ministry, although the ordination of women and enlistment of a self-sustaining ministry has, for the time being at least, helped to fill the gap.

However, as we have noted above, even more important than this demographic and economic decline, the church in the UK has lost sight

---

[1] See R. Katz et al. (eds), *Gen Z Explained: The Art of Living in a Digital Age* (Chicago: University of Chicago Press, 2021).

of the fact that the people of God in the world are its primary resource for mission. Clericalism, imprisoned within a parochial and pastoral model of church, remains embedded in every church. The church's retreat into the sphere of the local and the private, given impetus by the Enlightenment and the march of science and technology, has resulted in its engaging less and less with the concerns of society and the wider world.

More recently, the church in the UK, and far beyond, has suffered another huge body blow. Its past treatment of unmarried mothers and their children, and its inability to deal with child sexual abuse involving its clerical leadership, have taken a terrible toll on the credibility of the message of love as the heart of Christian faith. This makes it what Paul Avis calls "a counter-sign of Christ and of the kingdom of God".[2]

As I have noted in relation to the ecumenical movement, a further problem undermining the ability of the church to take a lead in responding to the communal needs of today is its continuing divisions. Werner Ustorf informs us that "Christianity today is split into approximately 34,000 separate denominations" and is now "a massive Babel of diversity".[3] Currently, divisions in the Eastern Orthodox Church, not least between its Russian and Ukrainian branches, exacerbated by nationalistic differences, have led to the dire consequences we are now seeing in Eastern Europe. Churches in the UK, United States and elsewhere continue to divide along ethical and biblical lines. The Roman Catholic Church is split between those supporting or opposing the reformist agenda of Pope Francis.

Nevertheless, despite the state of the church within Britain and beyond, the fact that it is still here speaks volumes for the tenacity of the Christian vision of "a new heaven and a new earth" with which it was originally endowed. Its kingdom-centred legacy, acknowledged or not, remains an invaluable resource for its own renewal and for the communal

---

[2] Paul Avis, *Reconciling Theology: Conflict and Convergence in Theology and Church* (London: SCM Press, 2022), p. 112.

[3] In Hugh McLeod and Werner Ustorf (eds), *The Decline of Christendom in Western Europe, 1750–2000* (Cambridge: Cambridge University Press, 2003), p. 220.

transformation of Western society and the wider world. The people of God still honour that legacy in many ways which offer a daily witness to the gifts of the kingdom community in action.

For that kingdom community to come in its fullness, it remains imperative for that Christian legacy not only to be sustained but developed further as a universal source of communal enrichment and power. There is no blueprint as to that legacy's ultimate nature and form. However, in the rest of this book I spell out what I believe to be a vision of a "new way of being church" and how the latter might again become the means of sustaining and developing that legacy. I am convinced that the church to come will have little to offer society and world if it focuses attention only on healing its own divisions, a weakness of Paul Avis otherwise powerful plea for "a reconciled church".[4] Its ultimate integrity and credibility depends on it embracing the divine imperative that the quest for community, the transcending of the communal dilemma and the creation of an inclusive global community of communities, is put at the heart of its mission.

What is now required to facilitate the salvation of church and world alike is the coming into being of a church inspired and empowered by the gifts of the kingdom community. The church is not that kingdom; it is the emissary or ambassador of that kingdom. From the perspective of this book, this means that its commission is to be the servant of the kingdom *community* and consequently of humankind. This means it is fundamentally a *diaconal* church.[5]

"A new era"

Our world is experiencing, as Pope Francis puts it, "a change of era". We have learnt that neither the homogeneity of Christendom nor the rationalism and heterogeneity of a post-Reformation world can suffice if we are to create a global community of communities which enables humankind and the planet to survive and flourish. A new era calls for a

---

[4] Avis, *Reconciling Theology*.
[5] For "Twenty theses describing the diaconal church", see Appendix 3.

renewed quest for community, espoused by church and society, and for a communal global culture.

To move on from the inadequate symbolic universes of the past and achieve that goal, the West, and wider world, will need to reclaim, make more clearly manifest and universalize the vision of its kingdom-centred Christian legacy. It will mean engaging in an institutionalization process which can move us away from insular values and norms, facilitating a new and inclusive "social construction of reality".[6] That "reality" has to be a world which has a greater potential than hitherto in history to enable its diverse communities to surmount the communal dilemma and create a global community of communities.

I am convinced that the task of discovering the meaning of a genuinely Christian symbolic universe, and what its institutions would look like, urgently needs a new impetus. Alasdair MacIntyre put it this way in the now classic ending to his book *After Virtue*:

> What matters at this stage (in our current quest for a more holistic moral order) is the construction of local forms of community within which civility and the intellectual and moral life can be sustained through the new dark ages which are already upon us … We are waiting not for a Godot, but for another—doubtless very different—St. Benedict.[7]

I believe it is no "slip of the pen" that MacIntyre here refers to a Christian symbolic figure, and the hugely influential movement of religious communities to which Benedict and his Rule gave such impetus some 1,500 years ago, as the kind of development now needed to motivate and empower our world to become a global community. I also believe that in this new era, it is the church, though in diaconal form as envisioned below, which still remains in pole position to inspire and help shape this new quest for community. This is because such a church has a Trinitarian

---

[6] P. Berger and T. Luckmann, *The Social Construction of Reality* (Harmondsworth: Penguin, 1966, 1984).

[7] A. MacIntyre, *After Virtue: A Study in Moral Theory*, 2nd edn (London: Duckworth, 1985), p. 263.

commission to further the transformational communal change of every institution, sacred and secular, on which the future of humankind and the planet now depends.

The meaning of *diakonia*

The meaning of the word *diakonia* has been vigorously debated over recent decades. Since its association in the early nineteenth century with the emergence of the Lutheran deaconess movement and the latter's works of caring and nursing, the concept has been taken to be synonymous with works of compassion and, not infrequently, with humble service. The growth of the ministry of the diaconate across most mainstream churches in subsequent years was consequently assumed to be about the importance of the church engaging in such "service" or "good works", especially amongst the poor and marginalized. This understanding of *diakonia*, now extended more widely to embrace human rights, justice and peace-making as in the World Council of Churches' recent document *Called to Transformation*, has remained the norm.[8]

However, in the early 1990s, John Collins, an Australian Roman Catholic scholar, after an exhaustive study of classical and biblical sources, concluded that the *diakon-* words did not originally have an exact meaning but gained this from the context in which they were set.[9] In the New Testament, therefore, *diakonia* did not normatively mean "charitable service" but whatever was the "mandate from a commissioning person or institution".[10] In the New Testament context, therefore, Collins argued that the primary focus of *diakonia* was not meant to be that of "service" as an action-focused undertaking, but that of "servanthood" as a person-centred relationship with the one doing the

---

[8] *Called to Transformation: Ecumenical Diakonia* (Geneva: World Council of Churches, 2022).
[9] J. N. Collins, *Diakonia: Re-interpreting the Ancient Sources* (New York: Oxford University Press, 1990).
[10] J. N. Collins, *Diakonia Studies: Critical Issues in Ministry* (New York: Oxford University Press, 2014), pp. 46 and 181.

commissioning.¹¹ This covered a diversity of mandates but notably that of being an emissary and including the role of spokesperson, ambassador, messenger, intermediary, go-between or agent.

As Paula Gooder argues, the key issue arising from this extremely important change of perspective is *who* is doing the commissioning and for *what* is the person commissioned? Gooder's conclusion is that the ultimate commissioning authority is God.[12] In the context of all that has been said hitherto, I contend that the ultimate commissioning authority is the Trinity, that divine community of Persons exemplifying community at its zenith.

In the New Testament, the word *diakonia* is nearly always used in connection with the internal life and leadership of the early Christian community.[13] However, as the church needed to engage with wider society, so did the implications of *diakonia* become more outward looking. In early nineteenth-century Europe, the church took to heart the commission (*diakonia*) to serve the poor and marginalized in the new industrial cities and the deaconess movement emerged in response. I argue that, in our day and age, the Trinity's commission is for emissaries who will further the communal transformation of human collectives through the gifts of the kingdom community. The means of undertaking this is for those so called to reflect the ministry of Christ who exemplified the nature of servant leadership and its kenotic demands.[14]

---

[11] David Clark, *Breaking the Mould of Christendom: Kingdom Community, Diaconal Church and the Liberation of the Laity* (Peterborough: Epworth Press, 2005), pp. 76–7.

[12] Paula Gooder, "Towards a diaconal church: Some reflections on New Testament material", in D. Clark (ed.), *The Diaconal Church: Beyond the Mould of Christendom* (Peterborough: Epworth Press, 2008), p. 102; and "Diakonia in the New Testament: A dialogue with John N. Collins", *Ecclesiology* 3:1 (2006), p. 37.

[13] A. Dulles, *Models of the Church* (London: Gill and Macmillan, 1974, expanded edn 2002), p. 93.

[14] Mark 10:45. N.B. Collins argues that the word "and" in this text points to the kenotic nature of Christ as "servant".

The diaconal church as institution and movement

Avery Dulles in his book *Models of Church*, quoting Paul VI, reminds us that "the church is a mystery... a reality imbued with the hidden presence of God. It lies, therefore, within the nature of the church to be always open to new and ever greater exploration".[15] Consequently, Dulles goes on to explore five models of church—as institution, mystical communion, sacrament, herald and servant, as well as their relation to eschatology. His purpose is not to decide which of these models represents "the true church"; it is to demonstrate that each model contributes to an ideal type though, on their own, each model has strengths and weaknesses.

One of Dulles' main contributions to our understanding of church is that he acknowledges that the models he identifies have emerged in response to cultural and social forces at work in particular periods of history, even when what has been discovered has continued to have meaning well into the future. For example, he associates the model of the church as "institution" with the political realities of certain eras from Constantine onwards. He sees the church as "mystical communion" harmonizing "with the general trend towards democratization in Western society in the eighteenth century".[16] As a Roman Catholic, Dulles is particularly aware that the Second Vatican Council has contributed to succeeding generations being "rocked by paradigm shifts" in their understanding of church.[17] This is notable with regards to *Lumen gentium* reaffirming "the idea that the church is the Body of Christ" and that "the principle paradigm of the church ... is that of the People of God".[18] Of note is the Council's affirmation of "the Pilgrim Church".[19] As well as the recognition, in its Decree on Ecumenism, of "a true though diminished realization of the Church of Christ in non-Roman Catholic communities".[20]

---

[15] Dulles, *Models of the Church*, p. 16.
[16] Dulles, *Models of the Church*, p. 28.
[17] Dulles, *Models of the Church*, p. 29.
[18] Dulles, *Models of the Church*, p. 48.
[19] Dulles, *Models of the Church*, p. 106.
[20] Dulles, *Models of the Church*, p. 134.

In what follows, I offer a different model of church, the diaconal church, which I believe to be a response to a radically new era which has begun to emerge in recent decades. It is a model which draws on features of all of Dulles' ideal types. The diaconal church is one commissioned by a Trinitarian God to work for the coming of the kingdom community by enabling all human collectives to be transformed by the gifts of life, liberation, love, learning and servant leadership. Only so can the communal dilemma be ultimately resolved, and a global community of communities come into being. I use the term "commission", rather than the word "mission", to emphasize that the meaning of *diakonia* in the New Testament is that of a person or collective receiving and fulfilling a *com*mission. In this sense, the mission of the diaconal church is always a "*com*mission".

The diaconal church is summoned to be the servant of the kingdom community. However, the diaconal church can never contain the kingdom. Charles Marsh writes: "We should not collapse the kingdom into the church, nor should we diminish the full energy of the church to radiate outward into a gathering more inclusive than the confessing body."[21] The diaconal church, as the Body of Christ, acts as the living exemplification of the kingdom community. Lesslie Newbigin notes that "without the hermeneutic of such a living community (the church), the message of the kingdom can only become ... an ideology and a programme; it will not be a gospel".[22]

To fulfil this commission, the diaconal church has been assigned two distinct tasks. The first is to identify, celebrate and ensure the continuity and development of its Christian heritage, embodied in the kingdom community and its gifts, in and through the life of *the church*. This is primarily a commission to the church as *institution* (unlike Dulles, I use the term institution more in a sociological than theological sense). As institution in my sense, the diaconal church contains many of the hall

---

[21] C. Marsh, *The Beloved Community: How Faith Shapes Social Justice from the Civil Rights Movement to Today* (New York: Basic Books (Perseus), 2005), p. 208.

[22] L. Newbigin, *Your Kingdom Come* (Leeds: John Paul, The Preacher's Press, 1980), p. 12.

marks of Dulles' models of institution and sacrament and, to a lesser extent, of mystical communion and herald. The church as institution also has an eschatological orientation which, as the Second Vatican Council's Decree on the Missionary Activity of the Church asserts, means that, after the gospel has been preached to all nations, it "will be gathered like a harvest into the kingdom of God".[23]

As institution, the diaconal church is commissioned to be the guardian of the West's Christian legacy, a symbolic universe embodied in the kingdom community and its gifts and handed down to succeeding generations across the centuries. Its responsibility is to "recapture the initial impetus" of the early church, commemorate the church's key traditions and build on that legacy.[24] The emphasis here is on continuity and sustainability. The diaconal church as institution is called to model and exemplify through its own life and work what it means to be a kingdom community so that the wider world can better grasp the meaning of the gifts of life, liberation, love, learning and servant leadership.

The other task is assigned to the diaconal church primarily as *movement*. It is a commission to discern and draw on the gifts of the kingdom community to further the communal transformation of *society* and *world*. Here the diaconal church reflects many of the features of Dulles' model of church as servant. He writes that "the Christian has a special vision of the inherent dignity of every human person, a distinctive ideal of unity and peace among all men, a unique concern for freedom, a singular confidence in the value of suffering and sacrifice, and an unequaled hope that in the end God will establish his kingdom in all its fulness". [25] Here the church becomes a communal change-agent.

These two tasks, continuity and transformation, are integral and complementary. Fulfilling both is imperative if the church is to honour its Trinitarian commission to be the servant of the kingdom community as well as that of humankind. A church which exists only as an institution will eventually find itself unable to adapt and develop. It will have less and less to offer a rapidly changing world and will eventually find itself

---

[23] Dulles, *Models of Church*, pp. 109–10.
[24] Avis, *Reconciling Theology*, p. 75.
[25] Dulles, *Models of Church*, p. 147.

ignored and redundant. It is only as it engages as movement, and learns to develop in the light of that calling, that it will be able to overcome the desire to defend rather than enrich, enhance and share its Christian heritage. At the same time, any new way of being church which attempts to operate only as movement may for a while appear to have the potential dynamism to further the communal transformation of society and world. However, if "the 'big bang'... that generated the church and its mission in the first place", as well as its Christian heritage, are forgotten or neglected, it will greatly weaken its power to make that transformation a reality.[26]

The diaconal church

Commission

To be the servant of the kingdom community and of humankind
To enable every human collective to be transformed
by and manifest the kingdom community's gifts of life,
liberation, love, learning and servant leadership

As institution	As movement
Continuity	Transformation

Primary resource

The people of God	The people of God in the world
"A royal priesthood"	A prophetic community

Form

The people of God gathered	The people of God dispersed
Communities of place	Communities of practice

Response to the gifts of the kingdom community

Empowerment

Worship and the sacraments, spirituality and prayer

Education

The theology of the kingdom community
The art of discernment and skills of intervention

Discernment

within the church and its locality	within society and world

---

[26] Avis, *Reconciling Theology*, p. 75.

Intervention	
For the communal flourishing of the church and its locality	For the communal transformation of society and world
Focus on communities of place	Focus on communities of practice
Nurture	
Wellbeing of the people of God	Wellbeing of the people of God in the world
Exemplification of the kingdom community	
The church as model	Every human collective as model

Leadership

Servants of the kingdom community
Collaborative

Presbyters	**Deacons**
An order of continuity	An order of transformation

Bishops
An order of unity

Governance

Self-governing—shared decision-making
—subsidiarity—partnership—ecumenism

The diaconal church as institution

Primary resource

For the diaconal church as institution, lay people are its primary resource. They are "a chosen race, a royal priesthood, a holy nation, God's own people that (they) may declare the wonderful deeds of him who called (them) out of darkness into his marvellous light" (1 Peter 2:9).

Form

As institution, the diaconal church remains primarily one where the people of God gather in communities of place to worship, learn and socialize. It is a church dominantly associated with the neighbourhood. As institution, the diaconal church gives physical expression to its identity through its buildings. In the UK, the parish church, the minster and especially the cathedral are for most people buildings which have for years symbolized the nation's Christian heritage.[27] As such they remain of considerable importance to many, churchgoers or not, within the neighbourhood concerned, bearing witness to the tenacity of the Christian legacy still present in Western culture.

Empowerment

In worship and the sacraments, the diaconal church as institution recalls and celebrates its Christian legacy, its Trinitarian sovereign and the gifts of the kingdom community. I have indicated earlier in this book how the key elements of worship give expression to those gifts. Spirituality and prayer here also come to the fore.

Education

The diaconal church as institution has the responsibility of enabling its members to understand as clearly as possible the nature and implications of a theology of the kingdom as a community on which its ministry and mission is founded. This means introducing its members to the Trinitarian foundations of that theology and the gifts of the kingdom community and their potential attributes. It will also entail exploring the way in which the life and teaching of Christ as described in the Gospels, in particular the parables of the kingdom, help to clarify the signs of the gifts of the kingdom community and throw light on their practical implications.[28] In this task the gift of learning, especially through its attributes of a quest for truth, attention and openness, is key. It enables

---

[27] As it has been down the centuries. See also David Clark, "The Church as Symbolic Place", *Epworth Review* 2:1 (1974), for other aspects of this designation.

[28] See Appendix 1 for the biblical underpinning of the gifts of the kingdom.

all those involved to see their education in the faith as an exciting and challenging journey of spiritual discovery.

Discernment

As institution, a primary responsibility of the diaconal church is to discern the ways in which the gifts of the kingdom community are being made manifest or are failing to be honoured within its own life as a gathered community. Such discernment requires an awareness of how the Christian legacy has shaped the church over history. However, just as Christ questioned certain religious traditions of his day, so the diaconal church seeks to discern where, in the past and present, the church as institution has got it "right", but also where it has got it "wrong", and sometimes very wrong.

As primarily a community of place, the task of the diaconal church as institution is also to discern where in its locality the gifts of the kingdom community are flourishing and where they appear to be weak or apparently absent.

The diaconal church recognizes that discernment is an art which is learnt over many years. At its heart is the ability to see and listen for signs of the gifts of the kingdom community at work in the world—as Christ put it, "Blessed are your eyes, for they see, and your ears, for they hear" (Matthew 13:16). Discernment also requires of the people of God that they discover an appropriate spirituality which can help them in this difficult and sensitive commission.

Discernment is not only an individual undertaking. Anna Rowlands states that Pope Francis sees "the discernment of the common good as a synodical process".[29] Christian collectives of all kinds have this commission. However, the way in which any kind of common mind is to be achieved needs careful professional and spiritual preparation by those in a leadership role. Discernment is an essential preparation for intervention.

---

[29] Anna Rowlands, *Towards a Politics of Communion: Catholic Social Teaching in Dark Times* (London: T&T Clark, 2021), p. 122.

Intervention

For the diaconal church as institution, the primary purpose of intervention is to enable every gathered congregation to be enriched by and manifest the gifts of the kingdom community. Where discernment reveals a church to be responding with awareness and faithfulness to those gifts, its task is to encourage and intensify their flourishing. Where discernment finds a church to be out of touch with or negating the gifts of the kingdom community, the task is to challenge and surmount that which is blocking those gifts coming to fruition.

The commission of the local church as institution is also to enable those collectives within its geographical orbit, and usually communities of place, to manifest the gifts of the kingdom community. This may likewise entail the church encouraging its people, as well as offering its premises, to further social, educational or welfare activities of a community-building nature.

The diaconal church as institution also has the responsibility of "planting" and sustaining "new" churches as and where needed to help ensure the continuity and sustainability of its own life and work as an institution. Such initiatives are often called "fresh expressions of church".

Nurture

The diaconal church as institution has pastoral responsibility and care for the wellbeing of its members and local residents in all aspects of their lives.

Exemplification of the kingdom community

The diaconal church seeks, as institution, to become a model of what it means to be commissioned as a servant of the kingdom community.

The diaconal church as movement

Mortimer Arias writes: "Jesus' call was to turn to God and his kingdom, present in him. It was an invitation to enter into a community and into a movement."[30] In the early Christian era, it was the church as movement which gave particular impetus to the transformation of the Roman Empire. However, once institutionalized, be it in the form of a "total institution" such as Christendom, or a plethora of "denominations" post-Reformation, the church as institution has always been in danger of introversion and stagnation.

Charles Marsh, referring to the writings of Victoria Gray Adams, writes:

> The kingdom of God originates in God's revolution which is movement in the most basic sense: God's own inner and eternal movement, the trinitarian movement which precedes and cuts through all human movements as their hidden history and momentum, the creative origin of all human movements towards human liberation and flourishing.[31]

Time and again, the church has needed to take the form of a movement in order to engage with a changing world. The commission of such movements, as in the case of many religious orders, has been to "speak truth to (ecclesiastical) power" and remind its own institutional leadership that it is not the kingdom but the servant of the kingdom.

The ongoing separation of church and state, the "secularization" of a Western world that was once regarded as a "sacred" society and the coming of an increasingly mobile and pluralistic world, given impetus by a digital revolution, has heralded a new era. Within it, communities of practice have become increasingly dominant. This means that the institutional church, as historically a community of place, has found it

---

[30] Mortimer Arias, *Announcing the Reign of God: Evangelization and the Subversive Memory of Jesus* (Philadelphia: Fortress Press, 1984), p. 112.
[31] Marsh, *The Beloved Community*, p. 211.

increasingly difficult to bring its influence to bear on many aspects of the life of society.

The church of the future, the diaconal church, now needs to engage credibly and effectively with a secular, cosmopolitan and mobile world. Consequently, it is imperative that, alongside retaining its form and function as an institution, the diaconal church assumes whatever form is needed to become once again a movement for communal transformation. What form might the diaconal church as movement take?

The people of God
In a secular and cosmopolitan world, it is the people of God *in the world* who are the core of the diaconal church as movement. Wherever they live, work or play, their call is to enable social collectives to make manifest and be transformed by the gifts of the kingdom community.

They are a prophetic community in the sense of "forthtelling" the presence of that kingdom.

Form
The people of God in the world are members of a variety of what I have called "institutional communities of practice". The latter proliferate within all sectors of society—from family life to the worlds of education, business and commerce, health and welfare, law and order, government and so on.

At the same time, the people of God in the world are also members of what I have termed "non-institutional communities of practice". These operate beyond the boundaries of established institutions. They are often focused on voluntary interests. However, they can also play a vital role in relation to economic, social and political issues of particular concern to a diaconal church seeking the communal transformation of society.

It is the active involvement of the people of God in such communities of practice which gives them the experience, insight and authority to bear witness to what the gifts of the kingdom community have to offer these influential spheres of public life. It is the insights and resources of the people of God active "in the world", where the kingdom community is already present and at work, that enable the diaconal church as movement to engage in its communally transforming mission.

Empowerment

As a dispersed community, members of the diaconal church as movement often find regular attendance at collective worship difficult. This makes it vital for the diaconal church to help the people of God *in the world* to develop a personal form of spirituality which can stand them in good stead in what can be a lonely situation or a hostile environment.

The diaconal church as movement is heir to a spirituality, perhaps witnessed most clearly in the life of the religious orders, themselves often taking on the character of the church as movement, which provides immense riches. Many of their members, from Julian of Norwich, through Ignatius Loyola, to Thomas Merton have offered forms of spirituality and rules of life still relevant to the ministry of the people of God in the world in a digital, mobile and fast-moving age. The forms of spirituality associated with the gifts of the kingdom community mentioned earlier in this book are another such resource. Other devotional practices[32] and prayers[33] are today available to provide support, guidance and encouragement to the diaconal church as a communal movement.

Education

The diaconal church as institution is mainly responsible for educating the people of God in the Christian faith, and in particular the meaning and significance of a theology of the kingdom community. For the diaconal church as movement, the educational task is focused on helping the people of God to understand the process of communal transformation and acquiring the knowledge, skills and experience needed to engage in that process. It is a task which requires not only the art of discernment but the ability and sensitivity to know when and how to intervene to bring the gifts of the kingdom community to the fore.

---

[32] For example, the Roman Catholic Church's Young Christian Workers' *Review of Life* based on Cardinal Cardijn's "SEE, JUDGE, ACT" method. <https://www.ycwimpact.com/>, accessed 12 May 2023.

[33] See David Clark, *The Kingdom at Work Project: A Communal Approach to Mission in the Workplace* (Peterborough: Upfront Publishing, 2014), pp. 296–321.

Discernment

Christ told the Pharisees that the "kingdom of God is not coming with signs to be observed" (Luke 17:20). On the other hand, to his disciples he said, "blessed are your eyes, for they see, and your ears, for they hear" (Matthew 13:16). And to all those listening attentively to his words, his guidance was "seek and you will find, knock and it will be opened to you" (Matthew 7:7–8).

Essential for the mission of the diaconal church as movement is its members' ability to discern the signs of where and how the Christian legacy, the gifts of the kingdom community, are present in daily life and work. Discernment is an art entailing the God-given ability to "see" and "hear" the signs of the gifts of the kingdom community all around us. It is an art which has to be learnt not least because those signs, as Christ indicated, are often small-scale, fleeting and associated with everyday happenings. At the same time, the art of discernment is also about recognizing where the gifts of kingdom community "appear" to be absent. I stress the word "appear" because the kingdom community is a tenacious community and, even in the most inhuman situations, as Martin Niemöller once reported from his experience of confinement in a German concentration camp, glimpses of its gifts can almost always be discerned.

As with the church as institution, discernment for the church as movement is not just the responsibility of individuals. Collectives, from small groups to large gatherings, will from time to time be called upon to discern the way forward. Ways in which all concerned can be fully involved in this process and a common mind reached demand servant leadership of a high order.

Intervention

As a movement, the diaconal church is committed to communal transformation. Consequently, it commissions the people of God in the world to exercise the role of change-agents. Wherever they are situated, this makes some form of intervention imperative. Because such intervention will mostly mean responding to everyday happenings, it will usually be spontaneous and direct. However, to bring about enduring change, more strategic forms of intervention may well be required. In the context of the workplace, I have elsewhere suggested several stages of planned intervention.[34] These are:

- the discernment of the presence or "absence" of the gifts of the kingdom within the social collective concerned
- in the light of this discernment, planning how and when to intervene to increase the influence of the kingdom community's gifts in those collectives
- building partnerships with others, Christians or not, committed to similar communal forms of change
- taking action to bring about communal transformation.

In relation to all forms of intervention, a word needs to be added here about the importance of what I call "mission as dialogue".[35] Thomas Thangaraj sums this up well:

> Dialogue is witness even without an evangelistic agenda. Seeing dialogue as a preparation for the announcement of the good news is misguided. In dialogue one lives out the good news that God accepts all as God's own children (*liberation*) ... In expressing our responsibility, solidarity, and mutuality with others (*love*) ... we are, in fact, making the good news present (*learning*) in the midst of dialogue.[36]

---

[34] I have described at some length the process of discernment and intervention for Christians at work in David Clark, *The Kingdom at Work Project: A Communal Approach to Mission in the Workplace* (Peterborough: Upfront Publishing, 2014). See also *The Kingdom at Work Project: A Handbook*, obtainable in digital form from rev.julian.e.blakemore@gmail.com.

[35] Clark, *The Kingdom at Work Project*, pp. 265–92.

[36] M. T. Thangaraj, *The Common Task: A Theology of Christian Mission* (Nashville, TN: Abingdon Press, 1999), p. 98. I have added in brackets the relevant gifts of the kingdom community.

One great asset of dialogue is that it opens the way to the resolving of "difference and disagreement (which) are absolutely integral to human existence and essential to life in community".[37]

Intervention of an even more comprehensive kind will be required to respond to issues or crises such as those indicated at the outset of this book. In any global context, groups of diverse kinds, some explicitly Christian, others not, will need to come together to form strong communal movements if they are to stand any chance of changing the values and norms on which our institutions are currently founded.[38] Here the prophetic voice of the diaconal church as movement is of critical importance in reminding our world that accessing the gifts of the kingdom community is imperative for the survival and flourishing of humankind (Matthew 16:24).

There are of course many situations where the gifts of the kingdom community are deliberately ignored. Human history is stained with the blood of millions, shed because of a thirst for power and glory by religious and secular leaders and collectives alike. Where the dark side of community rules, the world becomes a fragmented, frightening and hostile place. The communal dilemma is no abstract concept. Its tenacity can bring havoc in its wake. Here intervention to offer the gifts of the kingdom community not only requires considerable experience, skill and perseverance, it also requires great courage. The diaconal church does not dodge the fact that the ministry of the symbolic figure it worships led him to a cross.[39] However, it also believes that such suffering is the gateway to "a new heaven and a new earth" (Revelation 21:1) and that the fruits of communal transformation are worth all the cost.

---

[37] Avis, *Reconciling Theology*, p. 143.

[38] The history of the Trades Union Movement, in which many Christians were involved, is an example of this process.

[39] The implications of this are impressively described in Jürgen Moltmann, *The Crucified God: The Cross of Christ as the Foundation and Criticism of Christian Theology*, tr. R. A. Wilson and J. Bowden (London: SCM Press, 1973).

Nurture
The diaconal church as movement engages in the nurture of the people of God active in the world. This is especially important in situations where they encounter opposition or hostility, or their message is treated as irrelevant or dangerous.

Exemplification of the kingdom community
The diaconal church as movement exemplifies what it means to be a kingdom community in today's world. It is of little use being proactive in seeking to transform society if the medium is not the message. The people of God in the world are commissioned to demonstrate, by the way in which they live and bear witness to the gospel, that they are members of a kingdom community exemplifying the gifts of life, liberation, love, learning and servant leadership.

Servant leadership of the diaconal church

Every member of the diaconal church is potentially a leader, some within the church as an institution, others when it takes the form of a movement. All are called upon to exercise servant leadership.

However, the diaconal church recognizes that certain of its members are called to the three-fold order of ordained ministry as a tried and tested aspect of its Christian legacy. Because the titles of "presbyter", "deacon" and "bishop" have changed in meaning down the centuries, the diaconal church continues to reappraise the nature of these forms of ordained leadership in the light of the needs of today's world. In what follows, I retain the titles of the church's traditional three-fold order but identify some of the radical changes which the emergence of a diaconal church now makes imperative.

Within the diaconal church the three ordained forms of leadership are "full and equal orders", as James Barnett once put it. Leadership also remains collaborative. The working together of all those ordained to leadership, as well as in partnership with lay people, is imperative. Forms of collaboration will vary according to the circumstances, but all will essentially be different forms of team ministry.

Presbyters as "an order of continuity"

I use the term "presbyter" to indicate those traditionally described as ordained "to the ministry of Word and Sacrament". "Priest" is the alternative title in most pre-Reformation churches. The ministry of the presbyter remains of fundamental importance in supporting and sustaining the life and work of the diaconal church *as institution*. This means a radical re-orientation of their ministry.

Within the diaconal church, the presbyter is the main custodian of the West's Christian heritage, notably of its theology of the kingdom as a community and its implications for ministry and mission in today's world. This requires that the presbyter understands how that legacy has informed or failed to inform the life of the church down the centuries.

Within the diaconal church as institution, therefore, I identify presbyters as *an order of continuity*. Such a calling is far more significant than that of "maintenance". It is not about preserving past ways of being church for the sake of survival. It is a commission to discover new ways of discerning, accessing, celebrating, employing, and exploring further the kingdom community and its gifts, in order to enrich the lives and empower the ministry of the people of God in today's world.

The responsibility of the presbyter in the diaconal church is to help the people of God to own, affirm, celebrate and make manifest within their own lives the gifts of the kingdom community, and the Trinity as their source. The presbyter is also concerned that the gathered church exemplifies what it means to be the servant of the kingdom community through worship, learning, pastoral care and mission within the local area. The presbyter undertakes this task by exercising and exemplifying the role of servant leader.

The roles of the presbyter as servant leader—visionary, strategist, catalyst, intermediary, enabler, educator and partner—are focused on the life and work of the gathered church. The roles of visionary and catalyst are concerned with enabling the people of God to be inspired by and eager to make the vision of their church as a microcosm of the kingdom community a reality. The presbyter as strategist seeks out ways and means by which that undertaking can best be accomplished in the context of the situation and character of the congregation concerned.

As an enabler, the presbyter is responsible for nurturing and empowering the people of God for their ministry through affirmation of their abilities, encouragement of their endeavours and pastoral care. The presbyter's role as educator is concerned with encouraging and furthering the people of God's journey of discovery in the Christian faith, one especially focused on the nature and meaning of the gifts of the kingdom community—life, liberation, love, learning and servant leadership—and their implications for ministry in church and society.

The presbyter as partner is concerned to further ecumenical links with other churches and those agencies in the locality which are seeking to make manifest, consciously or not, the gifts of the kingdom community.

Being an order of continuity in no way excludes presbyters from being engaged in mission. Their contribution is "to grow" and develop the church as a community of place through endeavours such as "church planting" wherever necessary and feasible.

Because the experience, knowledge and skills required to fulfil this role are multiple, the presbyter will inevitably require the support, experience and skills of others, lay and ordained. Presbyters will, therefore, normally find themselves involved in team ministries, though frequently as team leaders.

Presbyters, *as an order of continuity*, have the privileged and vital task of ensuring that the diaconal church as institution preserves, celebrates and continues to build on its Christian heritage, embodied in the kingdom community and its gifts. The presbyter's role is to ensure that the medium, the gathered community as a key part of the institutional church, is the message. This means making certain that the diaconal church's worship, education, pastoral care, and its mission reflect its commission to be the servant of the kingdom community.

Deacons as "an order of transformation"

A glimpse of diaconal history

In the early church, the diaconate played an important part in leadership, exercising liturgical, educational, administrative and pastoral roles, often closely associated with the office of bishop. It was only after the Council of Nicaea (AD 325) that presbyteral ministry came to dominate that of the diaconate. "By the later medieval era the Latin or Roman rite had relegated the diaconate to a stepping-stone to the priesthood, which effectively marginalized the order for a thousand years", writes Michael Jackson.[40]

However, from the early nineteenth century onwards, and especially in the West, the diaconate has developed in a wide diversity of ways.[41] Jackson describes the current situation as follows:

> At one end of the spectrum would be the deacon as a liturgical functionary; at the other end, the deacon as an ecclesiastical social worker. The Eastern rites would be at the liturgical end of the spectrum, followed by the Roman Catholics; the Reformed Churches would be at the social work end, followed by the Lutherans. As usual, Anglicans would be somewhere in the middle![42]

Thus, today, we have one of the three historic orders of the church still searching for a clear role relevant to the current needs of both world and church.

A distinctive diaconate

I use the term "deacon" to indicate those who currently bear this title as "distinctive" deacons, that is those who are commissioned or ordained to a distinctive life-long office within the church. It is my contention that such a renewed "distinctive diaconate" is now of fundamental importance if the diaconal church *as movement* is to fulfil its vital ministry of

---

[40] D. M. Jackson, "The Diaconate in the Anglican and Lutheran Traditions: An Anglican Perspective", *Consensus* 43:1 (2022).

[41] D. M. Jackson (ed.), *The Diaconate in Ecumenical Perspective: Ecclesiology, Liturgy and Practice* (Durham: Sacristy Press, 2019), pp. 161–7.

[42] Jackson, "The Diaconate in the Anglican and Lutheran Traditions", p. 2.

communal transformation in society and world.⁴³ However, the issue of the so-called "transitional diaconate" needs to be addressed first.

Michael Jackson reminds us that the transitional diaconate is "typical of the Anglican, Roman Catholic and Eastern traditions—[being] the passage through the order of deacons [taken] for a year, more or less, [by] those to be ordained presbyter or priest".⁴⁴ This form of "sequential", and, later, "cumulative" ordination (the idea that "inside some deacons there is a priest, and inside some priests there is a bishop", as Rosalind Brown puts it⁴⁵), became common practice in the church from the fifth century onwards. Clearly, the concept of a transitional diaconate entrenches the assumption that the distinctive diaconate is "an inferior office".

Within the diaconal church, any prolongation of a transitional diaconate would be a hindrance to the emergence of a distinctive *and* renewed diaconate. Alison Peden puts her finger on the issue when she writes that "ordaining priests to the transitional diaconate is a challenge to the vocational integrity of deacons and their ordination. To spend months and even years carefully discerning a call to be deacon, a herald of the kingdom and a commissioned agent of the Church's mission, and then watch ordination to the diaconate being used as a stepping-stone rite for those without that vocation diminishes a role that God has created".⁴⁶ She goes on to argue that "as disciples and as ordinands, candidates should be directly ordained to either the diaconate or the priesthood as and when the Church is satisfied that they can respond to its call with integrity and competence".⁴⁷

---

43   David Clark, *Building Kingdom Communities: With the Diaconate as a New Order of Mission* (Peterborough: Upfront Publishing, 2016).

44   Jackson, "Introduction", in D. M. Jackson (ed.), *The Diaconate in Ecumenical Perspective: Ecclesiology, Liturgy and Practice* (Durham: Sacristy Press, 2019), pp. 2–3.

45   Jackson, "Introduction", p. 3.

46   Alison Peden, "Integrity of Vocation and the Transitional Diaconate", in D. M. Jackson (ed.), *The Diaconate in Ecumenical Perspective: Ecclesiology, Liturgy and Practice* (Durham: Sacristy Press, 2019), p. 48.

47   Peden, "Integrity of Vocation and the Transitional Diaconate", p. 50.

The "hidden diaconate"

I here focus on the role of a renewed distinctive diaconate. However, I believe that in the diaconal church those currently appointed by the church to undertake some form of society-focused ministry (for example, ministers-in-secular-employment, many chaplains, "mission enablers", "pioneer ministers" and so forth) should be seen as an integral part of a renewed diaconal order. This means that within the diaconal church there is a very large "hidden diaconate" waiting in the wings to swell the numbers of those formally commissioned to be deacons.[48]

At the present time, there is a growing awareness across many churches that a renewed diaconate has unrealized leadership potential of great importance for "the new era" ahead.[49] The problem is that, because many church leaders have thought little about what it means to be a diaconal church, and especially the complementarity of the church as institution and the church as movement, there is little understanding of the potential of a renewed diaconate or agreement as to what it should look like.

In exploring the ministry of a renewed diaconate, Michael Jackson's observation that the diaconate currently forms a spectrum of confusing diversity has to be taken as something of a complication. Nevertheless, despite the present kaleidoscope of diaconal roles and responsibilities, I believe it is increasingly clear what must be the role and responsibilities of a renewed distinctive diaconate within the diaconal church, the church to come.

An "order of transformation"

I regard a renewed diaconate as *an order of transformation*, one complementing that of presbyters as "an order of continuity". Representing the servant leadership of *the diaconal church as movement*, its primary commission is to work for communal transformation *within every sector of society*. In this task, it will seek to be alongside all those,

---

[48] See Clark, *Building Kingdom Communities*, pp. 137–9.
[49] See Jackson, *The Diaconate in Ecumenical Perspective*. See also David Clark and Maurice Staton, "Towards a renewed diaconate: Signposts from *The Diaconate in Ecumenical Perspective*" (2019), available at <https://sites.google.com/view/skdiaconate2018/articles>, accessed 12 May 2023.

Christian or of other convictions, striving to make manifest the gifts of the kingdom community.

At the same time, a renewed diaconate, as a communal movement, is commissioned to be an order of transformation *within the life of the church*. A renewed diaconate has the responsibility, exercising the role of servant leaders, to remind the church as institution that it is the servant of the kingdom community and also needs to be transformed by and manifest its gifts.

Diaconal leadership roles

In large part as a result of the seminal work of John Collins offering a new understanding of *diakonia*, understanding of the ministry of a renewed diaconate has now moved well beyond the traditional concept of "humble service". This transition in no way devalues the selfless service typical of the diaconal associations of Europe in the nineteenth century, and in many places still ongoing. Indeed, the call for the deacon "to pour himself/herself out in service to the outcast, the marginalized, the poor and suffering ... as Jesus did", as Gloria Marie Jones urges, is as crucial as ever.[50]

Nevertheless, the urgent task now is to relate the commission (*diakonia*) of a renewed diaconate as an order of transformation to the missional imperatives of the twenty-first century. In that context, the apostolate of a renewed diaconate is to fulfil the mission of the diaconal church and, therefore, to be focused on the building of kingdom communities within every sector of society. It needs to be stressed that this is a call to clear and significant leadership responsibilities.

A renewed diaconate's liturgical vocation

Within the diaconal church, a renewed diaconate's participation in worship would facilitate a sense of common purpose, colleagueship and

---

[50] Gloria Marie Jones OP, "Women and the Diaconate: A Roman Catholic Perspective", in D. M. Jackson (ed.), *The Diaconate in Ecumenical Perspective: Ecclesiology, Liturgy and Practice* (Durham: Sacristy Press, 2019), p. 153.

mutual support between the church as institution and the church as movement, between it being a community of continuity and a community of transformation.

When involved in the leadership of worship, a renewed diaconate's task is not to clone the role of the presbyter nor to take on the task of presbyter's assistant. It is to engage in those aspects of the liturgical life of the diaconal church which bring to the fore the Trinitarian commission to the people of God to be kingdom community builders in the life of society and world.

Rosalind Brown argues that, liturgically, a renewed diaconate is one which exercises "a ministry of hospitality" in preparation for, during and after worship.[51] She maintains that to focus the deacon's liturgical role on hospitality means that a deacon should be "on the church door to welcome and reassure people",[52] involved in the reading of the scriptures and the leading of intercessions, prepare the table for holy communion, and offer a dismissal which "orders rather than invites people to leave the church to live (out) in the world" that way of life embodied in the worship in which they have been engaged.[53] A renewed diaconate also has a responsibility to speak (preach) during worship about the insights they have gained whilst engaged in furthering the communal transformation of society.

Core leadership roles

In its leadership capacity as movement, a renewed diaconate has two core roles which are *church-facing*: **enabler** and **educator**, and three core roles which are *world-facing*: **catalyst, intermediary** and **partner**. The other roles identifying servant leadership—visionary and strategist—remain important and come into the picture as and when needed.

Which servant leadership role comes to the fore will be determined by the specific context within which deacons are working. In Appendix

---

[51] Rosalind Brown, "The Deacon in Worship: A Ministry of Hospitality", in D. M. Jackson (ed.), *The Diaconate in Ecumenical Perspective: Ecclesiology, Liturgy and Practice* (Durham: Sacristy Press, 2019), pp. 161–7.

[52] Brown, "The Deacon in Worship", p. 164.

[53] Brown, "The Deacon at Worship", p. 167.

4, in relation to my own diaconal experience, I offer some idea of how the empirical context shapes the roles required.

The deacon as enabler and educator

To equip the diaconal church as a movement for communal transformation, the key church-facing roles exercised by a renewed diaconate as servant leaders are those of *enabler* and *educator*.

A renewed diaconate as *enablers* seeks to bring into being a church that manifests the kingdom community's gift of liberation. This entails freeing lay people, the church's mission resource in today's world, to pursue ways in which the diverse communities in which they are involved can more fully manifest the gifts of the kingdom community.[54] For lay people, *institutional* communities of practice within the world of work will be especially important as a focus of their ministry.[55]

However, the role of a renewed diaconate as enablers will often open up the possibility of their supporting lay people in kingdom community building in *non-institutional* communities of practice focused on social and political issues and concerns.

In exercising the role of *educator*, a renewed diaconate engages lay people in a journey of discovery concerning the meaning and process of communal transformation. This means lay people acquiring a deeper understanding and experience of the kingdom community at work in the world. The deacon as educator encourages the questioning of evidence, the challenging of values and the testing out of received wisdom. Here the gift of learning comes to the fore.

The tasks of a renewed diaconate as enablers and educator will include:

- gathering the people of God as and when necessary, to reflect on their ministry in daily life

---

[54] Self-supporting deacons will usually have a personal mission responsibility in relation to the communal transformation of their community of employment similar to that of lay people.

[55] Clark, *The Kingdom at Work Project*, op. cit.

- inspiring them for their community building vocation in the wider world
- affirming, equipping and mentoring them for that calling
- encouraging them to share their experiences and insights with one another
- empowering them by means of access to spiritualities associated with the gifts of the kingdom community
- modelling for them what it means in practice to be a kingdom community.

The deacon as catalyst, intermediary and partner
To equip the diaconal church as movement, the key world-facing roles exercised by a renewed diaconate as servant leaders are those of *catalyst*, *intermediary* and *partner*.

Catalyst: I have argued that communal groups, especially *non-institutional* communities of practice, and the movements which give them coherence and influence, can be of vital importance in the communal transformation of societies, and the institutions which embody the latter's values and norms. Consequently, the role of a renewed diaconate as a *catalyst* should be to the fore in helping to further this institutionalization process. This means deacons engaging with, affirming and aiding the development of non-institutional communities of practice as an essential part of their ministry.

The role of catalyst will involve a renewed diaconate in a process of discernment and intervention. This needs to include deacons:

- identifying the issues being pursued by non-institutional communities of practice: for example, preventing pollution of the environment (life), alleviating drug abuse (liberation), meeting the needs of asylum seekers (love), or improving adult illiteracy (learning).
- discerning and drawing attention to the gifts of the kingdom community being employed by these communities of practice or movements.

- discerning what and how such communities and movements, Christian or otherwise, are making manifest or neglecting the gifts of the kingdom community.
- affirming and promoting their endeavours where those gifts are present; challenging their endeavours where those gifts are neglected.
- forging connections between communities of practice and communal movements so that they can more fully share their visions, experiences, insights and skills.
- encouraging such communities and movements to work as partners in addressing issues of common concern.

A renewed diaconate, for example, might work with groups and movements opposing the destruction of the planet (upholding the gift of life), encourage those confronting racism or gender inequality (employing the gift of liberation), support groups and movements opposing the ill-treatment of migrants (furthering the gift of love), spur on those seeking to confront fake news or indoctrination (offering the gift of learning), and affirm groups and movements challenging autocratic leadership (by upholding the gift of servant leadership). Deacons as catalysts might also align themselves with groups and movements confronting xenophobia or jingoism, in that process proclaiming the universality and inclusivity of the kingdom community.

Deacons do not remain secretive concerning the source of the gifts of the kingdom community. They measure their interventions by the words of Christ that "a sound tree cannot bear evil fruit, nor can a bad tree bear good fruit" and that "the sound" and the "bad" tree can be distinguished from one another by their fruits (Matthew 7:18,20). At the same time, they seek any opportunity and every way possible, not least by the quality of their life as an order and through "mission as dialogue", to "declare the wonderful deeds of him who called (them) out of darkness into his marvellous light" (1 Peter 2:9).

Intermediary: Another key role related to the ministry of deacons as servant leader is that of *intermediary*. This involves a renewed diaconate facilitating the networking of groups and movements working for communal transformation, Christian or secular, in ways which can release and enhance their community building potential. Often collectives engaged in this task lack either the imagination and motivation, or simply the time and energy, to share their insights, expertise and resources.

Deacons as intermediaries have the task of facilitating creative connections so that the work of those concerned can be enhanced and given greater dynamism. It is a role which reminds those involved in kingdom community building that it is an undertaking which must be open and inclusive. The deacon as intermediary also helps groups and movements to resolve those inevitable conflicts and disagreements which may disrupt their community building task. Here the associated skills of reconciler, mediator and negotiator come to the fore.

Partner: The deacon as *partner* co-operates with all those agencies working for the communal transformation of society and world. This means seeking a purposeful ecumenical partnership with Christians from every church and those of other faiths who are in any way engaged in the work of the communal transformation. It is also a role which requires deacons to enter into partnerships with secular groups, associations and movements which have a similar communal agenda.

Other leadership roles: As and when needed, the servant leadership role of *visionary* will also energize and inform the ministry of a renewed diaconate. The deacon as visionary is one grasped and inspired by the vision of a world communally transformed by the gifts of the kingdom community. It is a vision that not only imagines what such a world would look like but how that vision might be made a reality. As *strategist*, the deacon becomes an "organizational architect" who strives to ensure that such communal visions and their values inform and shape the practice of all those social collectives with which they are involved.[56]

---

[56] P. M. Senge, *The Fifth Discipline: The Art and Practice of the Learning Organization* (New York: Currency and Doubleday, 1990), p. 343.

A renewed diaconate as "a religious order"

Unless a renewed diaconate takes the form of *a religious order*, its contribution to the mission of the church as movement in the twenty-first century will be diminished. However, the nature and form of a renewed diaconate as a religious order needs to fit the nature of a new era and not attempt to clone the form of religious orders of the past.

There are already precedents for this. The British Methodist Diaconal Order is a religious community whose strength is enhanced by networking, regular face-to-face and virtual meetings, area groups and an annual convocation. Mutual pastoral support is very strong. Its members pray for one another on a regular basis using a prayer diary which has a photograph, the location and, expressed in brief, the particular concerns of each member of the order recorded. There is also a rule of life suited to the needs of the order.[57] Its members are male and female, single and married, and employed full-time or part-time by the church or secular agencies.

Other matters

Profile and formation

The members of a renewed diaconate will be both women and men, a development still not the case in the Roman Catholic Church where the former remain excluded for the time being. Its members will be married or single, of diverse ethnicities and may have varied gender orientations. They will be employed full-time or part-time by the church, or by secular agencies.

The selection and training of a renewed diaconate as an order of transformation is all-important. Diaconal formation should not try and clone that of presbyters who, as an order of continuity, have a very different role to fulfil within the diaconal church. The aim of such a diaconal curriculum is that deacons will have a thorough grasp of a

---

[57] On the British Methodist Diaconal Order as a useful model, see David Clark, *The Gift of a Renewed Diaconate—and the Contribution of British Methodism* (Peterborough: FastPrint Publishing, 2018).

communal theology of the kingdom, of the ecclesiology of the diaconal church and of its community-building mission.

Deacons as members of an order of transformation need to acquire the skills of servant leadership. This means a much more "professional" form of training, calling on secular experience and resources, and perhaps requiring some form of external accreditation. A renewed diaconate also needs to engage in relevant supervised practice. In-service development is essential and should be ongoing.

Deacons as members of secular communities of practice

Within the diaconal church as movement there will be deacons who continue to be employed, full or part-time, by secular bodies associated with the world of work. They may also have formal responsibilities within collectives associated with the voluntary sector. In this context, their calling remains that of exercising the servant leadership roles set out above whenever and wherever possible. However, because of their secular employment, their ministry may at times become more akin to that of lay people, that of furthering the communal transformation of the workplace through their personal discernment and intervention.

With a renewed diaconate the church is offered a new order of ministry which can liberate the people of God for their mission "to grow the kingdom", as Alison Peden puts it.[58] The birth of a renewed diaconate as *an order of transformation*, empowered by also being *a religious order*, offers the diaconal church a radically new form of leadership able to give fresh clarity and impetus to the life and message of the kingdom in today's fragmented world.

Bishops as "an order of unity"

In the diaconal church, bishops, alongside presbyters and deacons, are servant leaders. Their primary role is that of intermediary, though other servant leadership roles often come into play. One reason for this is that their responsibilities span the diaconal church as both institution

---

[58] Peden, "Integrity of Vocation and the Transitional Diaconate", p. 186.

and movement. Because bishops of the diaconal church represent the integrity of the diaconal church as institution and movement, and the "communal holiness or wholeness"[59] of church and world, I identify them as *an order of unity*.

Their commission is to ensure that the people of God are aware of their responsibilities as members of the church as institution, facilitating the continuity and celebration of the Christian legacy embodied in the gifts of the kingdom community. It is also to help the people of God understand and be equipped for their calling as members of the church as movement, engaging in the work of kingdom community building in society and world. These responsibilities alone require the bishop to be able to fulfil a diversity of roles associated with that of servant leader.

In the diaconal church, bishops have a special concern that presbyters and deacons in their care work together to further the communal integrity of church and society. They are committed to ensuring that the two orders understand and affirm one another's distinctive callings, presbyters as an order of continuity and deacons as an order of transformation. Bishops encourage the two orders to communicate clearly and openly, and share their experiences, insights, skills and resources. The bishop also has the responsibility of promoting the formation of team ministries made up of lay people as well as presbyters and deacons.

Bishops are charged with being the "official" voice of the diaconal church in the public realm. As symbolic figures, they represent the diaconal church, be it institution or movement, as the servant of the kingdom community and of humankind. Their commission is to enable church and society to manifest the gifts of the kingdom community—life, liberation, love, learning and servant leadership—as fully as possible. This means that their public calling is "to speak truth to power", not least on behalf of the poor, oppressed and marginalized, so that the communal dilemma can be resolved, and the coming into being of a global community of communities facilitated.

---

[59] David Clark (ed.), *Reshaping the Mission of Methodism: A Diaconal Church Approach* (Oldham: Church in the Market Place, 2010), pp. 167-91.

Governance

Modes of church governance are currently as diverse as ecclesial institutions themselves, although most of the latter remain deeply embedded in the mould of Christendom.[60] Over past centuries church governance has been shaped by a diversity of social and cultural factors, secular and sacred, the latter, as Paul Avis argues, being "Holy Scripture, ecclesiology, polity (and) church law".[61] That will continue to be the case. Thus, in considering the nature of governance of the diaconal church, our quest is not for some universal blueprint but that which accords with its communal foundations, sociological and theological, and its Trinitarian commission. These communal foundations accord with four core modes of governance: self-governance, democratic decision-making, subsidiarity related to integrity and partnership.[62] All need to operate in the context of ecumenism.

Self-governance

For many centuries after its initial institutionalization, the church strove to ensure that sacred authority took precedence over secular power, the former reaching its zenith during Christendom. Since then, certain churches, as with the Church of England, have sought to hold on to an "established" relationship to the state. Compelling arguments have been made for the value of establishment. For example, Lucy Winkett believes it facilitates speaking truth to power, offers "safe" spaces for debate about the values a society espouses, enhances political accountability and prevents the growth of politicized religious sectarianism of the kind witnessed in the United States in recent years.[63]

---

[60] See Clark, *Breaking the Mould of Christendom*, op. cit.
[61] Avis, *Reconciling Theology*, p. 92.
[62] I identify the British Methodist Church as offering an important model of the diaconal church in *Reshaping the Mission of Methodism and the Gift of a Renewed Diaconate*.
[63] <https://www.churchtimes.co.uk/articles/2022/27-may3-june/comment/opinion/platinum-jubilee-the-privilege-of-establishment-must-be-seized>, accessed 12 May 2023.

However, a church which lives by the state, dies by the state. As the secular state has come to dominate the political scene, established churches have had to respond, sometimes being able to hold on to their historic privileges, sometimes losing them. Because established churches are, by definition, reliant on the goodwill of government, they can become hesitant to challenge and over eager to collude with those in power. The stance of the German Evangelical Church in the 1930s, and the Russian Orthodox Church today, are two of such cases in point.

The diaconal church is the servant of the kingdom community, not of the state. It cannot rely on the state for assistance, financial or otherwise. It must be free to support or challenge the latter if it is to be an authentic witness to the gifts of the kingdom community. This requires that it be self-governing, taking full responsibility for its own life and work. One consequence would be that it becomes more not less effective as both institution and movement.

Shared decision-making

No form of government is perfect. There are times when a church espousing a benevolent clerical "autocracy" can appear to move faster and achieve greater cohesion than a church struggling with "democratic" decision-making. Christendom and the Reformation reveal the strengths and limitations of both models of decision-making. There will remain occasions when the church, as is the case with certain secular institutions, requires a "hierarchical" form of governance in order to respond effectively to some immediate need of the times. However, this should remain a temporary phenomenon and not be assumed to be the "given" form of church governance.

Because the people of God are the diaconal church's primary resource, their voice needs not only to be heard but heeded. This points in the direction of some form of synodical government being the most appropriate means of decision-making.[64] Democratic debate and decision making is one means by which the diaconal church is most likely to be

---

[64] I have argued that the British Methodist Church offers an important example of the practice of synodical government. Clark, *Building Kingdom Communities*, pp. 161–72.

able to bear witness to the gift of learning and become an open learning community.

It is no great surprise, therefore, to find the Roman Catholic Church currently engaged in a worldwide series of synodical gatherings, initiated by Pope Francis. This process is not only intended to offer the church guidance as to its future but to test out the efficacy of a form of consultation and decision-making in which clergy and laity as the whole people of God debate and decide important issues. Anna Rowlands believes Pope Francis has a view of such synodality as a form of "collective discernment ... (which can offer) a vision for social as well as ecclesiastical judgement".[65] This is, she argues, "a turn towards political ecclesiology".

Subsidiarity

Subsidiarity is an organizing principle states which that all important decisions ought to be made at the "lowest level" of democratic government competent to deal with them. It is a key concept within Roman Catholic Social Teaching. In 1996, the Roman Catholic bishops of England and Wales stated:

> The twin principles of solidarity and subsidiarity need to be applied systematically to the reform of the institutions of public life. The protection of human rights must be reinforced, the mechanisms of democracy repaired, the integrity of the environment defended.[66]

In relation to subsidiarity in the life of the church, Paul Avis writes:

> The language of hierarchies of levels is invidious and ecclesiologically toxic ... The "higher levels" are not there to serve

---

[65] Rowlands, *Towards a Politics of Communion*, p. 103.
[66] *The Common Good and the Catholic Church's Social Teaching: A Statement by the Catholic Bishops' Conference of England and Wales* (London: The Catholic Church's Bishops' Conference of England and Wales, 1996), para. 119.

themselves, though there is a kind of entropy in all institutions that tends in this direction. Subsidiarity in the church means that lay people (though never without their pastors) provide the centre of gravity, the focus of discernment, for all that is discussed, debated and decided in a church.[67]

The diaconal church takes this stance as normative. However, it does not mean any abrogation of responsibility by those with overall authority. As Paul Avis argues, it simply means that the latter's power should always take the form of servant leadership.

Pope Francis has described "subsidiarity as a principle of hope".[68] However, it has been questioned whether "the 'positive' and 'negative' elements of subsidiarity are fully integrated in papal teaching".[69] For example, Rowlands points to the fact that in Roman Catholicism there is a "failure to integrate women fully into decision-making and governance roles" in the church. And the limited commitment to genuine synodality in numerous churches reveals there is still a good way to go.

Partnership

It follows from this that the diaconal church is committed to work together with any human collective, whether Christian or based on other faiths, convictions or none, which seeks to bring to the fore in whatever form any of the gifts of the kingdom community. Such partnership, especially between churches, takes the form of what in recent decades has come to be known as "the ecumenical movement".

---

[67] Avis, *Reconciling Theology*, p. 87.
[68] Rowlands, *Towards a Politics of Communion*, p. 235.
[69] Rowlands, *Towards a Politics of Communion*, p. 236.

The ecumenical imperative

All that I have written about the nature, mission, ministry and governance of the diaconal church underlines the fact that such a church exemplifies what it means to be "one universal church renewed for mission". This is true of its inner life. It means that the diaconal church as institution *and* as movement is one church, though with complementary modes of expression. It means that the laity and the ordained leadership of such a church see themselves as one people of God. It means that those in leadership roles work collaboratively and operate as teams. It means that disagreements and disputes are wherever possible settled "out of court" and not allowed to undermine the fundamental communal values and principles on which the diaconal church is founded.

The essentially holistic nature of the diaconal church does not mean the creation of some homogenous global entity. Diversity and difference are essential, not least to honour the gift of liberation which enables each person and collective to attain its own distinctive identity. The gift of learning here also comes to the fore, not least because it facilitates dialogue and enables people to appreciate and accept that different cultural and ritual expressions of the Christian faith can enrich not divide the one church. Where there are the inevitable breakdowns of relationship, the gifts of kingdom community can together pave the way for reconciliation, that process of opening up to one another, recognition of other churches as also part of the people of God and the renewal of strong communal bonds. This process of reconciliation, Paul Avis sees as at the heart of what Christian faith has to offer to a fragmented church and world.[70]

Because the word *oecumene* means literally "the entire human community", the ecumenical imperative also means that the diaconal church seeks to be in partnership with all those seeking to create a diaconal world, one which serves the kingdom community and seeks to manifest its gifts.

---

[70] Avis, *Reconciling Theology*, pp. 196–238.

The diaconal church—its global commission

The diaconal church is the servant of the kingdom community. It is a kingdom-centred church. It does not exist for itself. Nor, as with "established" churches, does it exist to further the wellbeing of any particular nation. Its commission (*diakonia*) is to enable every human institution to manifest the gifts of the kingdom community. Its mission is to witness to the gospel of universal communal wholeness or holiness.

It is a commission which the Christian church has been seeking to fulfil for two millennia. It has often failed to recognize or to be true to that calling. Progress has sometimes been excruciatingly slow. Frequently the vision of the kingdom as a community has succumbed to a "vision" of humanity's self-centred power and glory. "The state we're in" may seem to suggest that little has changed. Nor does "the state the church is in" appear to offer great encouragement. In particular, the church's neglect of itself as movement is critically undermining its mission. Nevertheless, over the centuries, a Christian legacy—incarnated in the kingdom community and its gifts—has slowly permeated the "Western mind",[71] communally transforming its culture, shaping its institutions and paving the way for the eventual creation of a global community.

At this *kairos* moment in history, when the crises facing humankind could well be terminal, I believe that a new kind of church, the diaconal church, is being called into being to make that legacy plain, to celebrate it and to help humanity build upon it. The importance of such a church is out of all proportion to its size. Obsession with the survival and growth of an anachronistic and clericalized institution simply delays this vital transition.

What matters is that the message of the diaconal church becomes prophetically clear. First, that the only communal "Reality" which can surmount the communal dilemma, overcome the destructiveness of closed and self-centred human institutions and bring one world into being is that of the kingdom community and its gifts. Secondly, that because the source of the power of the kingdom community is that of the

---

[71] Tom Holland, *Dominion: The Making of the Western Mind* (London: Abacus, 2019).

Trinity, of divine providence, that community offers the genuine hope of "a new heaven and a new earth" (Revelation 21:1) coming into being.

As *institution*, the diaconal church has been entrusted with the task of enabling its members to know what it means to be fully alive; to be liberated from self-centredness and to live for others; to offer unbounded compassion for the poor and marginalized; to learn how to live well together; and to be guided by servant leaders. As institution, the diaconal church celebrates and maintains this legacy. As a community of place, the diaconal church cares for those for whom locality remains deeply meaningful. In fulfilling these institutional responsibilities, the leadership of presbyters as an order of continuity is vital.

As *movement*, the diaconal church equips the people of God in the world to enable the diverse communities of practice to which they belong to be transformed by the gifts of the kingdom community. It prepares them to discern and work alongside groups and movements, sacred and secular, which, consciously or unconsciously, are engaged in nurturing the gifts of live, liberation, love, learning and servant leadership. To further the mission of the diaconal church as movement, the leadership of a renewed diaconate as a new order of transformation has a crucial part to play.

The diaconal church, commissioned to be the servant of the kingdom community, offers a model for the institutions of society and world. It seeks to exemplify the meaning and nature of the communal task for all diaconal institutions. These have the responsibility for ending the communal dilemma and furthering the coming of a global community of communities.

The diaconal church, like all institutions, is fallible. It can neglect its commission. However, it stands as a symbol of a Christian heritage which was bequeathed to the West and now to a wider world, a symbolic universe which is the exemplification of community at its zenith and has the power to make that vision a reality.

The diaconal church knows that because of this Christian legacy, whether openly recognized or not, millions of people are in practice acting as servants of the kingdom community (Matthew 25:31–46). As in the positive responses to climate change, Covid-19 and to the suffering of those in Ukraine, acts of selflessness and compassion are everywhere in evidence. An impregnable kingdom community is already at work attending to the needs of a world in peril. It is empowering women and men everywhere to love their neighbours as themselves, and even to bless those who curse them (Matthew 5:44). The diaconal church does not hide its light "under a bushel" (Matthew 5:15). It is an open and active pointer to the source of this power for good, stirring people to recognize and claim the gifts of a loving and intimately engaged Trinity.[72]

The diaconal church seeks to stand as a bulwark against human evil, that which denies or neglects the gifts of the kingdom community. It is a church which knows that at the heart of the divine response to a fallen world is a cross, a counter-cultural sign of redemptive love, and the only abiding answer to institutional closure and selfishness. It is not a naïve church with visions that are utopian. It recognizes that "a new Jerusalem" is a costly city to build. However, it remains true to its commission to inspire and resource "from the highways and byways", within every nation and across all cultures, those prepared to have a go at building it. Because it is a church which recognizes that, in the end, there can be no truly diaconal world until every human institution, sacred and secular, becomes a microcosm of the kingdom community.

---

[72] For further reflection on this theme, see Clark (ed.), *The Diaconal Church*, pp. 173–211.

1 0

Creating a diaconal world: Diaconal institutions

In this book, I have argued that in order to address the potentially terminal challenges facing humankind, the communal dilemma has to be addressed and a genuine search for a global community begun. This will entail a new cycle of communal institutionalization. It is my belief that this "quest for community" needs to be shaped and empowered by a Christian symbolic universe incarnated in the kingdom community and offering to humankind the latter's gifts of life, liberation, love, learning and servant leadership.

In practice, this means humankind identifying, affirming and following those symbolic figures who embrace a vision of our common humanity and one world. It means our commitment to supporting communal groups which, by manifesting the gifts of the kingdom community, point us, in however modest ways, towards that end. It means encouraging and learning from any communal movement which enhances and furthers the endeavours of such groups. And, ultimately, it means institutions, great or small, taking the gifts of the kingdom community into their system and becoming *diaconal* institutions, servants of the kingdom community and of humankind.[1] The goal is the creation of "a *diaconal* world".

---

[1] I remind the reader that I define an institution as "an established organization which embodies the key functions, values and norms of a society as an enduring social, cultural and economic entity".

Primary and communal tasks

Before I explore the nature and form of the diaconal institution, I need to distinguish between two kinds of task which shape the purpose and form of any human collective: its primary task and its communal task.[2] A collective's *primary task* is that which it must fulfil in order to accomplish *the purpose for which it was established*. A school needs to educate, a hospital must heal, a police force has to maintain law and order and a business must produce and market goods or services. A primary task, which is clear and agreed from the outset, amongst other important features, is important if a collective is to retain its original identity.

If a collective is to become a *diaconal* collective, its primary task needs to be complemented by what I call its *communal task*. The latter is the task of *manifesting the gifts of the kingdom community*—life, liberation, love, learning and servant leadership. This means that the diaconal collective is working for the communal transformation of its own life and work, as well as of any other collective with which it might come into regular contact.

The communal task impinges on the life and work of a diaconal collective in two main ways. First, it is instrumental in shaping the overall purpose of the collective by ensuring that its primary task accords with the values embedded in the gifts of the kingdom community. The *diaconal* school, the diaconal hospital, the diaconal police force, the diaconal business and so forth, are social collectives whose primary task (education, healing, maintaining law and order, producing goods or services . . .) is being fulfilled and, *alongside that*, their communal task which makes manifest the gifts of the kingdom community. However, in the case of all collectives, it is important to question whether their primary task (for example, the production of weapons of war, of cigarettes, of fossil fuels or of chemical fertilizers) accords with or undermines their communal task.

---

[2] See also Appendix 3, "Twenty theses for the diaconal institution".

Secondly, in a diaconal collective, the communal task—the manifestation of the gifts of the kingdom community—will permeate and transform the social, cultural and economic life of the collective as a whole. This means the communal task will influence every aspect of the collective's life and work in relation to major decisions as well as those informal human transactions that are very important in the community building process.

A key difference between the diaconal church and many other diaconal collectives is that, in the case of the former, the communal task—building kingdom communities—is its primary task. Consequently, in the case of the diaconal church, the communal task becomes the primary task as well. In the case of other diaconal collectives, the two tasks will remain much more distinct, even though integrated.[3]

All that I have said above about primary and communal tasks in relation to human collectives applies equally to those collectives which are called institutions, to which I now turn.

Explicit and implicit commitment to a Christian heritage

There are institutions which by the very nature of their primary task find themselves explicitly committed to operationalizing the values and norms of a Christian symbolic universe. For example, schools, universities and hospitals which are identified with a particular Christian church, especially in the USA but also, notably in the case of schools, in the UK.

However, many such institutions are finding it harder, or less appropriate, to witness to an *explicit* acknowledgement of their Christian origins in a multi-faith and multi-cultural world, not to mention one now economically dominated by the norms of a market-driven symbolic universe. At the same time, many institutions now exist which have no knowledge of, or *overt* commitment to reflecting, the values and norms of a Christian symbolic universe. Nevertheless, as I have argued throughout this book, the West retains a Christian heritage which still permeates a good deal of the life of society as a whole. This means that many institutions in the UK, such as the National Health Service, can

---

[3] See David Clark, *Schools as Learning Communities: Transforming Education* (London: Cassell, 1996), pp. 38–9, 101–3.

be regarded as implicitly diaconal. What I suggest below, therefore, are some principles and practices typical of diaconal institutions which may be upheld, explicitly *or* implicitly.

The quest for community
The diaconal institution is committed to the quest for community within its own life and that of the wider world. The Christian symbolic universe which inspires and drives the diaconal church similarly inspires and drives the diaconal institution. The sociological and theological components of community underpinning that quest remain the same. Likewise, though diaconal institutions have a diversity of primary tasks to fulfil, the imperative of the communal transformation of their own life and that of society is the same.

Key features

Institution and movement
As with the diaconal church, diaconal institutions need to embrace "continuity" *and* "movement". The former (the institution as continuity) refers to the need for the institution to honour its past, and not least its primary task. The latter concerns its endeavours to respond openly and innovatively to a rapidly changing environment.

Flexibility
The diaconal institution as continuity needs organizational structures which offer it endurance in the midst of a changing world. In particular, it needs to safeguard those values of the West's Christian heritage which are important for its own life and work and those of the wider world. The diaconal institution as continuity often takes on the features of a community of place. This is because it usually needs some form of physical base to give it an ongoing identity.

The diaconal institution as movement needs to be able to disperse its members (workers, employees, personnel, etc.) in order to engage with wider society. This is necessary for it to be able not only to sustain its primary task but, in the process, enable it to fulfil the wider implications of its communal task. To address these responsibilities, it will usually consist of a wide diversity of communities of practice.[4]

Primary resource
The diaconal institution, like the diaconal church, regards its members as its primary resource. It looks upon each as having a distinct and invaluable contribution to make to the life and work of the whole endeavour.

Empowerment
The way in which the diaconal institution empowers its members to fulfil its communal task is often revealed through its mission statement which, explicitly or implicitly, embraces the values of the kingdom community. Examples from the world of work might include:

- Life is Good: To spread the power of optimism.
- IKEA: To create a better everyday life for many people.
- JetBlue: To inspire humanity—both in the air and on the ground.
- Workday: To put people at the centre of enterprise software.
- Prezi: To reinvent how people share knowledge, tell stories, and inspire their audiences to act.
- Tesla: To accelerate the world's transition to sustainable energy.
- Invisible Children: To end violence and exploitation facing our world's most isolated and vulnerable communities.

Education
The diaconal institution as continuity educates its members in an awareness and appreciation of ways, past and present, in which it has sustained its primary and fulfilled its communal task. As movement, it equips them with the resources, knowledge and skills to continue to develop its communal purpose in today's world.

---

[4] E. Wenger, *Communities of Practice: Learning, Meaning and Identity* (Cambridge: Cambridge University Press, 1998) and E. Wenger et al., *Cultivating Communities of Practice: A Guide to Managing Knowledge* (Boston, MA: Harvard Business School Press, 2002).

Discernment and intervention

For the diaconal institution, the practical aspects of community building are similar to those I have described for the diaconal church. Because the gifts of the kingdom community are always present throughout the life of society, they will also be available to enhance the life of the diaconal institution. Building the latter as a microcosm of the kingdom community becomes, as with the church, a matter of both discernment and intervention. In relation to discernment, the question is to what extent the institution is life-giving, liberating, loving, a learning community and how it exercises servant leadership? In relation to intervention, the question is deciding what action members of the institution need to take to make possible greater openness to the gifts of the kingdom community.

For the diaconal institution as movement, the process of discernment and intervention is again similar to that of the diaconal church. Here, however, the focus is on how, in the process of delivering its primary task, the institution can be engaged in the communal transformation of wider society. In the case of the diaconal institution as movement and, therefore, its greater contact with a multicultural world, its members will need considerable empathy and respect for the convictions and views of all those with whom they are dealing. In this process dialogue becomes especially important.

Nurture

The diaconal institution as a whole has a deep concern for the health and welfare of its members. Its commitment to its members' wellbeing and that of their families will be evident in the quality of the human relationships built and the facilities and support offered to any in personal need.

Exemplification

As with the diaconal church, the medium of the diaconal institution as a whole needs to be its message. It should mirror the Trinity's communal image, whether recognized as such or not, and to manifest the gifts of the kingdom community. In this way its communal reputation may become an example which others are inspired to follow.[5]

Servant leadership

The literature on leadership, including that of institutions, is massive. However, in this book I am concerned with what Christian faith is able to contribute to the exercising of leadership which can enable humankind to surmount the communal dilemma, build a global community of communities and address the crises our world now faces. Because servant leadership is a concept which typifies the ministry of Christ, as well as reflecting the kind of authority exercised by the Trinity, it is a core gift of the kingdom community. The primary concern of servant leadership within the diaconal church is the education and empowerment of the people of God in the world. I believe that the concept of servant leadership, with its associated roles of visionary, catalyst, strategist, enabler, intermediary, educator and partner, represents the Christian contribution to all institutions, sacred or secular.

Forms of servant leadership
As with the diaconal church, diaconal institutions need three forms of servant leader each with their own distinct responsibilities. As with presbyters in the diaconal church, the diaconal institution requires leaders who are concerned about the preservation and continuity of the institution's heritage. This means enabling members to fulfil the institution's primary task and further its communal task in the light of that heritage.

There need to be other leaders, akin to deacons in the diaconal church, responsible for the institution as movement, engaging with a much wider

---

[5] In the nineteenth century, this was the case with a number of UK companies founded by Christian entrepreneurs such as Jeremiah Coleman (a Baptist and later Congregationalist), George Cadbury (a Quaker), Titus Salt (a Congregationalist) and William Hartley (a Methodist).

world in order that the institution may effectively fulfil and develop its primary and communal tasks more fully in relevant and dynamic ways.

The diaconal institution also requires a third form of leadership, akin to that of bishops in the diaconal church, which represents the holistic nature of the institution, co-ordinating and furthering the contributions of the other two aspects of leadership.

The autocratic norm
The exercise of servant leadership, in both world and church, is in stark contrast to that which has typified the form of leadership exercised by the leaders of most institutions down the centuries. Autocratic (or oligarchic) and hierarchic ways of controlling state, church and secular institutions have throughout history been normative. However, since the Second World War, the number of institutions embracing servant leadership has grown apace.

Nonetheless, over the last decade or so the number of nations opting for autocratic leadership has begun to increase, once again bringing a threat to the democratic constitution of even countries like the United States. The proliferation of autocratic styles of leadership is indicative of nation states where a significant proportion of the population are persuaded that their traditional way of life is being threatened, often because of an increasing influx of those from other cultures or religions. Autocratic leadership may appear to offer such nations a sense of security. In reality, it chokes off the gifts of the kingdom community, makes the communal dilemma all the more difficult to resolve, thwarts the creation of a global community of communities and makes it impossible to deal with crises threatening the future of humankind.

Governance

The economic context
I have not considered at any depth in this book how the coming of a Christian symbolic universe, and its embodiment in the kingdom community, might challenge the values and influence of the economic symbolic universe, that of the market, currently dominating the world

scene.⁶ It is true that the market economy has brought immense benefits for humankind. It has introduced a way of sharing goods and services that is able to cope with the complexities of globalization and the speed with which institutions must operate if the daily needs of billions are to be met. It has lifted many people out of poverty and enabled many others to live a secure, healthy and enjoyable life.

Nevertheless, a market economy has many communal flaws. Capitalism, on which it is founded, certainly has more than the "seven toxic assumptions" which Eve Poole describes.⁷ It is now evident that market globalism is failing to meet the needs of a new era. It has not prevented the rise of some very wealthy and other extremely poor nation states. It has not prevented the groundswell of displaced persons, in particular economic migrants seeking to earn a decent living for themselves and their struggling families.⁸ As Michael Sandel puts it, the needs of a global community cannot be adequately met within an economic symbolic universe wherein "everything is up for sale".⁹

The framework for a new form of a global economy which honours and employs the gifts of the kingdom community is not yet clear. However, the foundational gifts of the kingdom community are a given, some of which are reflected in Catholic Social Teaching. It is imperative that work continues on the nature of an economic model which can foster and underpin a just global community.

Self-governing
Like the diaconal church, the diaconal institution needs to be self-governing if it is to have the freedom to put into practice the principles on

---

6   In *The Kingdom at Work Project: A Communal Approach to Mission in the Workplace* (Peterborough: Upfront Publishing, 2014), pp. 84–102, I explore what "a communal economy for the world of work", an economic model based on the gifts of the kingdom community, might look like.
7   Eve Poole, *Capitalism's Toxic Assumptions: Redefining Next Generation Economics* (London: Bloomsbury, 2015).
8   See J. R. Saul, *The Collapse of Globalism* (London: Atlantic Books, 2018).
9   Michael Sandel, *What Money Can't Buy: The Moral Limits of Markets* (New York: Farrar, Straus and Giroux, 2012), p. 3.

which a communal theology of the kingdom is based. Nevertheless, there may be certain sectors of the life of society—health, welfare, education, transport, law and order—where it is more effective if the nation state has overall control. Even here, however, the diaconal institution working within the orbit of state oversight should be given the maximum opportunity to order its own affairs.

Shared decision-making

Much of what I have set out above about the nature of diaconal institutions, sacred and secular, shows that any moves towards shared decision making give the greatest hope of empowering people to work together to build communal institutions and a global community. Nevertheless, democracy, like all forms of governance, has inbuilt weaknesses. For example, democratic decision-making can be slow and turgid. It can bring stalemate where a near balance of power makes decision-making difficult, as currently in the United States. Unless shared decision-making respects the views of minorities, as well as recognizing the will of majorities, it can create closed and exclusive social systems. Even more dangerous, a democratic form of voting can open the way to authoritarian regimes gaining control and manipulating the system of government to retain power permanently, as in the case of Germany in the 1930s.

Nevertheless, as Churchill said in a speech on the House of Commons in 1947, "There is the broad feeling in our country that the people should rule, and that public opinion expressed by all constitutional means, should shape, guide, and control the actions of Ministers who are their servants and not their masters." Democratic decision-making affirms the dignity of every individual, enables people to break clear of immature dependency on autocratic figures or regimes, but also requires those concerned to take responsibility for the destiny of humankind. This accords with a Christian symbolic universe and the nature of a kingdom community which is about not only gifts but the responsibility to employ them wisely.

Subsidiarity

Anna Rowlands in her review of Catholic Social Teaching states that:

> ... within the texts of the (papal) encyclicals, the principle of subsidiarity focuses on people and their relationships—and participation in—social, political and economic groups and associations. Such groups might include everything from trade unions, local government, faith organizations, craft associations, football clubs, political parties, grassroots movements for social change to professional bodies of nurses or business entrepreneurs, women's institutes, social enterprises and charitable bodies. These intermediary associations, groups and institutions are referred to as the vital organs of 'social governance' ... These are the face to face, dispersed groupings through which society is enabled to reach its common good ... (They are) the organs of subsidiarity ... These groups fulfil a shared good and responsibility that exceeds them. For this reason, closed groups that become breeding grounds for abuse of every kind are in no sense a legitimate expression of subsidiarity.[10]

She continues:

> ... in an ideal scenario the state is envisaged as an engaged player, an active enabler of subsidiarity. Enabling power to flow in a dispersed way through plural smaller scale bodies fosters social creativity and human dignity in the life of organizations and groups. This constructive or 'positive' understanding of the principle of subsidiarity is balanced in the encyclicals by a more 'negative' emphasis on subsidiarity as a principle concerned with the limits of states and market powers.[11]

In this context, the diaconal institution is one in which its members, as individuals or institutions, most affected by any proposals for change are those given most sway in the decisions which have to be made about them. This is because the communal attribute of human dignity requires

---

[10] Anna Rowlands, *Towards a Politics of Communion: Catholic Social Teaching in Dark Times* (London: T&T Clark, 2021), pp. 227–8.

[11] Rowlands, *Towards a Politics of Communion*, p. 228.

that the voice of those most closely associated with the institutions involved in change should be listened to and respected.

Partnership
The diaconal institution is an open institution and a learning community. Such an institution, like the diaconal church, recognizes that it can never have the resources or skills to go it alone.

Consequently, partnership is of the essence of the life and work of the diaconal institution.

The vision and imperative of a diaconal world

The imperative quest for community which I have argued for and described in this book necessitates the creation of diaconal institutions and a diaconal world, shaped and empowered by a Christian symbolic universe. This is an immense undertaking. It is no wonder that again and again humankind has interpreted the quest for community in an introverted and closed sense, with the power of community used only to advance the interests of this or that self-contained group, institution or nation.

However, no institution, from the family to the nation state, can any longer be an island. It has never been more urgent that humanity recognizes that every time a country closes its borders, the ultimate future of humankind is put in grave danger. Furthermore, attempting to make any nation "great again" by devaluing other nations is a recipe for global disaster. Opting for Brexit in the name of an anachronistic imperialism, bestowing power on a Donald Trump with that slogan as his mission statement, pursuing the mirage of a "Holy Rus" through the invasion of Ukraine, or creating a doctrinaire and closed Chinese communist party in order to build an all-powerful nation, are signs of a world heading for self-destruction.

Nevertheless, human history remains shot through with positive and powerful signs of the kingdom community at work. A Christian symbolic universe, still struggling to emerge, continues to offer not only hope to a world in crises but the Trinitarian power of a divine community to make that hope a reality. For their salvation, the people of Israel were urged to "choose life" (Deuteronomy 30:19). Humankind, for its salvation and flourishing, is now being called to choose not only life, but liberation, love, learning and servant leadership, the universal and inclusive communally transforming gifts of the kingdom community.

Nothing less can suffice to save a world in peril. Deny life, and climate change will make the planet uninhabitable. Deny liberation, and those discriminated against on the basis of race, religion or gender will not only suffer but ultimately cause chaos. Deny love, and the poor and marginalized will in the end overwhelm the world with their cries for help. Deny learning, and indoctrination and "fake news" will exacerbate fear and prejudice. Deny servant leadership, and autocracy will infantilize and divide.

For our world to survive and flourish, the coming of the kingdom community is not a utopian vision but a communal imperative.

APPENDIX 1

Biblical references for attributes of the gifts of the kingdom community

The gift of life

Security
Christ told us not to be anxious about what we shall eat, drink or wear but to seek God's kingdom first "and all these things shall be (ours) as well" (Matthew 6:31,33).

Health
Christ healed many who were physically or mentally ill. In doing so, he stated that "the kingdom of God has come upon you" (Matthew 12:28; and Matthew 4:24; Mark 6:56).

Vitality
Christ said that he had come so that we "may have life, and have it abundantly" (John 10:10).

Creativity
Christ commended those entrusted with money by their employer who use or invest it wisely, and criticized anyone who hides it away for safe keeping (Luke 19:12–17).

Care of the planet
God entrusts the future of the planet to humankind (Genesis 1:28).

The gift of liberation

Significance
Christ taught that God was like a shepherd who was ready to risk his life to rescue a solitary sheep which has strayed away from the main flock (Luke 15:3–7).

Human dignity
Christ taught that not even a sparrow falls to the ground without God noticing, and that human beings are more valuable than many sparrows (Matthew 10:29–31).

Equality
Paul stated that "there is neither Jew nor Greek, there is neither slave nor free, there is neither male nor female; for (we) are all one in Christ Jesus" (Galatians 3:28).

Justice—restorative
Christ told a story of the son who suffered destitution because he wasted his share of the family inheritance yet, when repentant, was warmly welcomed back by his father (Luke 15:11–32).

Justice—distributive
Christ challenged the rich to share their wealth (Mark 10:17–25), and all of us to give of our possessions to those less well off (Luke 12:33). This was to follow his own example (2 Corinthians 8:9).

Forgiveness
A woman who, according to Jewish law should have been stoned to death for adultery, was forgiven by Christ (John 8:3–11).

Reconciliation
Paul writes that Christ came to bring human beings back into a living and loving relationship with God and, at the same time, with one another (2 Corinthians 5:17–20).

The gift of love

Solidarity
Christ prayed that humankind "may be one" (John 17:21).

Compassion
What Christ called "the great commandment"—the purpose of life is to love God and to love our neighbour as ourselves (Mark 12:29–31; Matthew 22:38–9; Luke 10:27).

Empathy
Paul wrote that love is patient, kind, not arrogant or rude, does not insist on its own way, is not irritable or resentful, celebrates what is right not wrong, believes and hopes and endures all things (1 Corinthians 13:4–7).

Caring
Christ told a story of a Samaritan who took care of a man of a different culture who had been robbed, beaten and left for dead (Luke 10:25–37).

Sharing
Matthew recounts a story of how Christ fed a large crowd which had come to hear him by enabling a small boy to share his lunch with everyone (Matthew 14:13–21).

Generosity
Christ said, "If anyone would sue you and take your coat, let him have your cloak as well ... Give to him who begs from you, and do not refuse him who would borrow from you" (Matthew 5:40–2).

The gift of learning

Socialization
Christ argued that he had not come to abolish the Jewish law and the message of the Old Testament prophets but to show what it really meant to live by the spirit and not the letter of that law (Matthew 5:17).

A quest for truth
Christ taught his followers that "When the Spirit of truth comes, he will guide you into all truth" (John 16:13).

Attention
The Bible gives examples of many experiences which, if we are "attentive", can reveal the glory of God. Some are "peak" experiences; for example, the spectacle of a "burning" bush (Exodus 3:2) or the majesty of the heavens (Psalm 19:1). Others are more common experiences such as the wonder of pro-creation (Psalm 139:13–16) or the beauty of "the lilies of the field" (Matthew 6:28–9).

Openness
One of Christ's longest and most challenging conversations was with a woman from a quite different culture (a Samaritan) (John 4:7–28,31–7).

Questioning assumptions
Christ encouraged his listeners to re-examine their approach to Sunday observance (Mark 2:23–8; 3:1–6), to question the importance of wealth (Mark 10:17–31; Luke 12:13–21), to review their response to the faults of others and, most challenging of all, to examine how well they treated their enemies (Matthew 5:38–42; 43–8).

Person-centred
Whether Christ was conversing with individuals or large crowds, it was their daily concerns which were the focus of his teaching. For example, the hazards for a farmer of sowing seed (Mark 4:1–20), the reaction of a shepherd to losing a sheep (Matthew 18:12–14) and the response of a father to a son who has gone astray (Luke 15:11–32).

The gift of servant leadership

There are a number of roles which the servant leader, as exemplified by Christ (Philippians 2:7), needs to play. Their biblical underpinning is illustrated below.

Visionary (All 4Ls)
Christ sets out his mission to help the marginalized and oppressed (Luke 4:18).

Strategist (All 4Ls)
Christ indicates to his followers what will be the final stages of his life's work (Matthew 16:21).

Catalyst (All 4Ls)
Christ throws dishonest money changers out of the Jerusalem temple (John 2:13–16).

Intermediary (Love)
Christ shows his followers how to enter into dialogue with people who have a different culture and faith (John 4:27).

Enabler (Liberation)
Christ commissions his followers to engage with others on his behalf (Mark 6:7).

Educator (Learning)
Christ teaches his followers how to pray (Matthew 6:7–13).

Partner (Love)
Christ seeks the colleagueship of all who espouse the kingdom—"He who is not against us is for us" (Mark 9:40).

APPENDIX 2

Twelve signs of the human city[1]

1. A human city is committed to being a new kind of city

A human city is a place alive with the energy of hope, enables imagination and creativity to flourish and looks for the revitalization of every aspect of its corporate life.

It is a city which is a dynamic community of communities that offers a powerful sense of security, significance and solidarity to all its members.

It is *a rainbow city* which delights in diversity and difference in pursuit of the common good.

It is a city which creates a new culture and a new language to embody and communicate what it means to be human.

A human city enables those who share a vision of the human city to work together with others to make that vision a reality.

2. A human city is committed to all those who live and work there, or visit it

A human city is about "value for people" before value for money.

It is a city where *all matter and each counts*.

It is a city where people acknowledge and respect one another, where they care and where they share.

---

[1] David Clark, *Building the Human City: The Origins and Future Potential of the Human City Institute (1995–2002)* (2011). Available at <https://humancityinstitute.wordpress.com/reports/>, accessed 9 May 2023.

3. A human city is committed to affirming the whole of human experience

A human city treasures the human achievements of its past and celebrates the human endeavours of the present.

It is a city committed to human wealth creation.

It is about the fulfilment of all that it means to be human in body, mind and spirit.

It is a city with a heart and a soul.

It is a compassionate and "faith-full" city.

It is a place of fun and laughter.

4. A human city is committed to a life-enhancing environment

A human city gives life to those who live and work there, or visit it.

It is a safe, clean and healthy city.

It is a city within which people can move about easily and comfortably.

It is full of natural beauty and architectural grace.

It harnesses and uses all its resources in ways that sustain the planet.

5. A human city is committed to social justice

A human city recognizes, repents and confronts the suffering that inhumanity causes.

It places the concerns of the poor and the marginalized high on its agenda.

It is committed to the vision of a just, peaceful and inclusive city, revitalized by forgiveness and reconciliation.

It upholds human rights and human responsibilities.

6. A human city is committed to truth and integrity in public life

A human city fosters a culture of trust founded on mutual respect and honesty.

It is about open, informative and straight communication within all spheres and at all levels of city life.

7. A human city is committed to the transforming power of the human group

A human city is dependent on a multitude of human groups contributing in their own ways and situations to the creation of the human city.

It is a city where "small is beautiful".

It values the human scale and the human touch.

It is a city with a human face.

8. A human city is committed to being a place of lively and creative encounters

A human city provides spaces and places where people can meet and talk.

It encourages those who live and work there to come together to share their experiences, stories and concerns.

It provides forums for vigorous discussion and debate about the meaning and nature of the human city.

It fosters many forms of networking that can link and connect those striving to build the human city.

9. A human city is committed to genuine partnership

A human city recognizes that the humanity of the part and the humanity of the whole are inextricably linked.

It is a city which brings together diverse sectors (public, private and voluntary), neighbourhoods, cultures, faiths and generations in innovative and creative ways.

It is a city which fosters the commitment, empathy, tolerance and tenacity which all true partnerships require.

It is a city which works with any other urban community that shares its vision.

10. A human city is committed to democratic leadership and participation

A human city gives its citizens a voice and hears what they say.

It enables its members to participate in the decisions that affect them.

It is a city which believes in the mutual accountability of those who live and work there, or visit it.

It is a city where those who lead use their power to empower others.

11. A human city is committed to learning for living

A human city is a learning city.

It is a city involved in an ongoing quest to discover what it means to be human.

It is a city which creates a multitude of opportunities for attentive listening, innovative exchanges, open dialogue, ongoing reflection and the birth of new understandings.

It is a city which provides an education for life.

12. A human city is committed to ongoing change

A human city is about fundamental and continuing change because its concern is the transformation of the inhuman into the human.

It is a city which never ceases to challenge and redeem those things which would destroy its humanity.

APPENDIX 3

Twenty theses for . . .

Twenty theses for the diaconal church

The global context
1. In the century ahead humankind faces *crises which could be terminal*.
2. If it is to survive, humankind needs to become *a global community of communities*.
3. Consequently, *the quest for community* must become a global imperative.

The kingdom community
4. *The Christian vision of "the kingdom community"* is the supreme exemplification of community and a model for world and church.
5. *The gifts of the kingdom community are life, liberation, love, learning and servant leadership*. They are gifts manifest within the life of the Trinity and in Christ's teaching about the kingdom of God. They are *universal* and *inclusive gifts*.

Commission
6. The com*mission* of the church is to build communities that manifest and are transformed by the gifts of the kingdom community. *The credibility* and *viability* of the church depends on how faithfully it fulfils this mission.

Servant

7. This mission can only be fulfilled if the church becomes *a "diaconal" (or servant) church*. The diaconal church is *the servant of the kingdom community* and *of humankind*.

Model

8. The diaconal church *exemplifies the meaning of community* for church and world.

The people of God

9. The diaconal church *liberates the people of God* to be the servants of the kingdom community in church and world.

Discernment and intervention

10. The mission of the diaconal church is undertaken by its *discerning* where and how the gifts of the kingdom community are affirmed or ignored, and by *taking appropriate action* in response.
11. For the diaconal church *dialogue* is a fundamental means of fulfilling its commission.

Form

12. The diaconal church takes *two forms*:

    - As *institution* and primarily *a community of place*—the Christian community *gathered*
    - As *movement* and primarily *communities of practice*—the Christian community *dispersed*

Leadership

13. To equip the people of God to be the servants of the kingdom community *new forms of church leadership* are needed. These are embodied in the role of *servant leader*.
14. The ordained leadership of the diaconal church is exercised through three offices:
    a. that of *presbyter* whose commission is:

i. to enable the gathered church *to identify, understand, celebrate, develop and communicate the meaning and implications of its communal heritage*, primarily as a community of place.
   ii. to enable communities (predominantly of place) located within the neighbourhood to manifest the gifts of the kingdom community.
  b. Presbyters constitute *an order of continuity*.
  c. that of *deacon* whose commission is:
   i. to enable the people of God in the world to be servants of the kingdom community, primarily as communities of practice.
   ii. to enable communities (predominantly of practice) in the life of society to manifest the gifts of the kingdom community.
  d. Deacons constitute *an order of transformation*.
  e. that of *bishop* whose commission is:
   i. to support and co-ordinate the ministries of presbyter and deacon and, through them, that of the people of God.
  f. Bishops constitute *an order of unity*.
15. The leadership of the diaconal church is collaborative.

Governance

16. The diaconal church is *self-governing*.
17. The diaconal church operates through *shared decision-making*.
18. The diaconal church embraces *subsidiarity* and *integrity*.
19. The diaconal church is committed to *partnership*.
20. The diaconal church regards the coming into being of one church and world (*oikoumene*) as a divine imperative.

Twenty theses for the diaconal institution

The global context
1. In the century ahead humankind faces *crises which could be terminal*.
2. If it is to survive, humankind needs to become *a global community of communities*.
3. Consequently, *the quest for community* must become a global imperative.

The kingdom community
4. *The Christian vision of the kingdom community* is the supreme exemplification of community and a model for world and institution.
5. *The gifts of the kingdom community are life, liberation, love, learning and servant leadership.* They are gifts manifest within the life of the Trinity and in Christ's teaching about the kingdom of God. They are *universal* and *inclusive gifts*.

Primary and communal commission
6. Alongside *the primary task* for which it was established, the *communal task* of every institution is to build communities, beginning with itself, that manifest and are transformed by the gifts of the kingdom community. *The viability* of the institution depends on how faithfully it fulfils both tasks.

Servant
7. An institution's communal task can only be fulfilled if it becomes *a diaconal (or servant) institution*. A diaconal institution is *the servant of the kingdom community* and *of humankind*.

Model
8. The diaconal institution *exemplifies the meaning of community* for society and world.

Members of the institution
9. The diaconal institution *liberates its members* to be the servants of the kingdom community in the world.

Discernment and intervention
10. The commission of the diaconal institution is undertaken by its *discerning* where and how the gifts of the kingdom community are affirmed or ignored, and by *taking appropriate action* in response.
11. For the diaconal institution *dialogue* is a fundamental means of fulfilling its commission.

Form
12. The diaconal institution takes *two forms*:
- as a means of continuity and primarily a community of place—its members gathered.
- as a movement and primarily communities of practice—its members dispersed.

Leadership
13. To equip its members to be the servants of the kingdom community *new types of institutional leadership* are needed. These are embodied in the role of *servant leader*.
14. The leadership of the diaconal institution is exercised through three key roles:
    a. that of *enabling the institution* (predominantly *as a community of place*) to fulfil its primary and communal task.
    b. that of *enabling the institution* (predominantly as *communities of practice*) to fulfil its primary and communal task.
    c. that of *co-ordinating* the leadership of those focused on the institution's primary and communal tasks as communities of place and practice.
15. The leadership of the diaconal institution is collaborative.

Governance
16. The diaconal institution is *self-governing*.
17. The diaconal institution operates through *shared decision-making*.
18. The diaconal institution embraces *subsidiarity*.
19. The diaconal institution is committed to *partnership*.
20. The diaconal institution is committed to the creation of one world.

APPENDIX 4

The deacon in action—a personal perspective

The best way I can illustrate the servant leadership roles of a renewed diaconate as an order of transformation is to draw on my own experience. I describe below in note-form some of those endeavours through which I have been able to play servant leadership roles. All involved discerning where the gifts of the kingdom community were already operative, or being neglected, and intervening in response.

At the time of the first three initiatives, I was a Methodist presbyter in the UK. However, I now believe that the roles which I played in those situations were fully diaconal. As one consequence of that conviction, I later moved from being a Methodist presbyter into the Methodist Diaconal Order, the first presbyter in the British Methodist Church to do so. As an ordained deacon, I headed up the other three initiatives described below.

I had the privilege of time and space to undertake the first three projects because I was employed by Westhill College, Birmingham, a church college of higher education, which acted as a supportive "umbrella" organization. However, I was still required to fulfil my responsibilities as a full-time lecturer in community education. The last three projects I undertook as a retired deacon. All the projects were based in the UK although they created many contacts with people elsewhere, especially in the United States.

The Christian community movement (1970-2003) embracing:

The National Centre for Christian Communities and Networks (NACCCAN) (1981-8)
becoming
The National Association of Christian Communities and Networks (NACCAN) (1988-2003)

Category: Groups (networks) and a movement
The time involved: 1970-88

My roles: visionary, strategist, catalyst, intermediary and partner. To affirm, build into a movement and help to resource a wide diversity of Christian communities and networks which had come into existence, explicitly or implicitly, to further one or more of the gifts of the kingdom community.

Status: A registered charity.

Location and staff: Rooms in Westhill College. Myself as Co-ordinator and then Director of the Centre (voluntary, then part-time paid, 1984-7), with one full-time and one part-time administrative staff members.

Participants: Representatives of 106 lay Christian groups and networks, and 42 religious orders (Roman Catholic and Anglican), attended a first national congress in 1980. A directory produced at that time listed some 250 lay groups and 130 religious orders.

Gatherings: National congresses in 1980 (250 attendees); 1984 (250 attendees); 1987 (200 attendees). Regional group meetings from time to time.

Oversight of NACCCAN/NACCAN: A group of trustees. A management committee made up of representatives of the groups and religious orders involved.

Links with the institutional church: Management committee chaired by the Bishop of Birmingham. Generally minimal interest and support from the wider church.

Funding: Grants from independent charitable trusts.

Methods of sustaining, developing and publicizing the movement: A regular "community" magazine, which I edited, and a "directory" of groups; a resource centre containing material about communities and networks across the UK; publications (see below); numerous journeys I undertook across the UK, and to Ireland and the USA, during college vacations to visit, affirm and connect groups and networks.

Continuation after I moved on: NACCAN continued to be run by a management committee, an administrator and a voluntary Moderator. Its location moved from time to time, usually to where the Moderator was based. Its magazine and directory continued to be published. NACCAN was formally wound up in 2003, by which time the community movement of the 1970s and 1980s had lost its original momentum.

Relevant publications:

Basic Communities: Towards an Alternative Society (London: SPCK, 1977).

The Liberation of the Church: The Role of Basic Christian Groups in a New Re-formation (Birmingham, Westhill College: The National Centre for Christian Communities and Networks, 1984).

Yes to Life: In Search of the Kingdom Community (London: Collins, 1987).

Breaking the Mould of Christendom: Kingdom Community, Diaconal Church and the Liberation of the Laity (Peterborough: Epworth Press, 2005), pp. 150–69.

The Christians in Public Life Programme (CIPL)

Category: *Individuals and groups*

The time involved: 1991–2001

My roles: enabler, educator and partner—"To achieve a new quality of public life by enabling Christians to engage, share and work together with others in addressing fundamental questions of common concern", not least those challenges caused by the domination of an all-pervasive market culture.

Status of the project: A voluntary initiative.

Location and staff: Westhill College. Myself as Co-ordinator (voluntary).

Participants: Mostly ordained ministers, and members of religious orders, representing a wide range of groups and associations sympathetic to the programme's purpose of enhancing the Christian contribution to public life.

Gatherings: Day events and two residential conferences, each with 40 people in attendance.

Oversight: An ecumenical steering committee of representatives of Christian groups engaged in issues of public life.

Links with the institutional church: The steering committee included an Anglican and Roman Catholic bishop (the latter with responsibility for his church's engagement in public life), a Methodist Chair of District, and Moderators of the United Reformed Church and Baptist Churches in the West Midlands. However, generally limited interest and active support from wider church.

Funding: Self-supporting—subscriptions and donations.

Methods of sustaining, developing and publicizing the movement: I commissioned and edited over 200 "position" papers (1,500 words each), widely circulated, and intended to help set an agenda for the church in public life. No such agenda was then in evidence. A regular newsletter.

Continuation after I moved on: None.

Relevant publications:

Changing World, Unchanging Church? (London: Mowbray, 1997).

Breaking the Mould of Christendom: Kingdom Community, Diaconal Church and the Liberation of the Laity (Peterborough: Epworth Press, 2005), pp. 170–87.

The Human City Initiative and Institute (HCI)

Category: Individuals, groups and collectives

The time involved: 1994–2000

My roles: visionary, strategist, catalyst, intermediary and partner—"To enable those who share a vision of Birmingham as a human city to work together with others to make that vision a reality." HCI's strap line: "All matter; each counts."

Status of the project: An "Initiative" which became an "Institute" with charitable status in 1997.

Location and staff: Initially based at Westhill College, Birmingham. Myself as Director before 1997 (unpaid), after 1996 an honorarium. One full-time and two part-time administrative staff (paid). Three neighbourhood project workers (see below).

Participants: A wide diversity of people from every sector across the city of Birmingham. The project began as a Christian initiative but soon embraced those of other faiths and convictions.

Gatherings: Public "hearings" in the town hall about what it meant to be a "human education system", "human business world", "human health service" ... A later more local series of "hearings" focused on what it meant to be a "human school", "human hospital", "human neighbourhood" etc.

Human city sites: Any group offering itself as making a practical contribution to the creation of a human city. Training and resource sessions for such sites.

Projects: "A Human City Youth Project" bringing together young adults and city leaders to share their hopes for the future of Birmingham.

"A Human Neighbourhood Project" to strengthen the sense of community in three disadvantaged neighbourhoods in Birmingham, Bradford and Swindon. One full-time project worker appointed for each neighbourhood. "Market places" in the cities concerned to show off what the sites were doing.

Oversight: Trustees and a governing council, the latter made up of representatives from a range of Birmingham agencies.

Links with the institutional church: Little interest or support from church leaders and local churches especially after the range of participants broadened well beyond those associating with the church.

Funding: Grants from independent charitable trusts. Funding from Government for the Human Neighbourhood Project.

Methods of sustaining, developing and publicizing the project: A regular "Human City Bulletin" going three times a year to some 3,000 people. A series of "Futures Papers" on what makes a city human. A human city website.

Continuation after I moved on: Three other Directors of the Institute followed. The last of these changed the nature of the project into an urban "think tank" and publisher of research papers, notably on social housing and multicultural issues.

Relevant publications:

Breaking the Mould of Christendom: Kingdom Community, Diaconal Church and the Liberation of the Laity (Peterborough: Epworth Press, 2005), pp. 188–209.

The Diaconal Church: Beyond the Mould of Christendom (Peterborough: Epworth Press, 2008), pp. 209–10.

Building the Human City: The Origins and Future Potential of the Human City Institute (1995–2002) (2011). Available at <https://humancityinstitute.wordpress.com/reports/>, accessed 9 May 2023.

The Bakewell Community Project—Building Bridges

Category: Individuals and groups

The time involved: 2012–14

My roles: strategist, catalyst, intermediary and partner: To engage all sectors and organizations in Bakewell in building new or stronger bridges across every sphere of town life, and between Bakewell and the wider world. A focus on initiatives which manifested practical expressions of one or more of the gifts of the kingdom community.

Status of the project: A voluntary initiative.

Location and staff: Bakewell, Derbyshire. Myself as Co-ordinator (voluntary).

Participants: All those concerned, Christians or otherwise, living or working in Bakewell.

Gatherings: Public displays in the Methodist church of what the town was doing across all sectors—business, health, education, welfare, voluntary bodies, etc.

Oversight: The Association of Bakewell Christians (Anglicans, Roman Catholics, Methodists and Quakers).

Links with the institutional church: The local churches in Bakewell were all fully supportive and actively involved. No church interest beyond Bakewell.

Methods of sustaining, developing and publicizing the movement: Organizations (churches, traders, shops, schools, voluntary groups, etc.) became "Community Sites" (and received a certificate to display) by pledging to work at one bridge-building initiative during 2013. Pledges were publicized in a regular *Bakewell@Work Newsletter* and through displays in the Bakewell Co-op.

In 2014, to keep the momentum going, renewed and new pledges were grouped under *"Ten visions" for Bakewell and beyond*:

1. The great workplace! Businesses as community builders
2. All matter—each counts! Caring for those 'on the edge'
3. Getting together! Harnessing the power of gathering
4. Life begins at 80! Enriching life for those in our residential homes
5. Learning for living! Pursuing a life-long journey of discovery
6. Arts for all! Engaging every generation
7. Going green! Maintaining a sustainable and beautiful planet
8. Working together! Hands across the town
9. In the know! Keeping everyone in touch
10. A just world! Meeting the needs of the poorest.

Continuation after I moved on: None.

Relevant publication: The Kingdom at Work Project: A Communal Approach to Mission in the Workplace (Peterborough: Upfront Publishing, 2014), pp. 356–8.

The Kingdom@Work Project

Category: Individuals and groups
The time involved: 2014–21

My roles: enabler, educator and partner—To enable Christians "to transform the world of work through a process of discernment, partnership and action, informed and empowered by the gifts of the kingdom community (life, liberation, love, learning and servant leadership)".

Status of the project: A voluntary initiative.

Location and staff: Managed mostly "online" from my home in Bakewell with myself as Co-ordinator (voluntary).

Participants: Christian individuals and representatives of groups and associations committed to bringing their Christian faith to bear on and help transform the world of work.

Gatherings: Two major conferences in Birmingham and several consultations involving the participants indicated above.

Oversight: A close and ongoing partnership with St Peter's Saltley Trust, Birmingham.

Links with the institutional church: Mainly through gatherings such as those noted.

Methods of sustaining, developing and publicizing the movement: The project commissioned and edited 15 extended *Bulletins*, many containing articles written by the members of faith and work associations, on such themes as: Servant leadership, Spirituality in the workplace, Chaplains and chaplaincy, Christian faith and the economy, etc. All the *Bulletins* are available from the St Peter's Saltley Trust's website and downloads have run into the hundreds for each *Bulletin* (see below).

In 2021, the project and the trust produced a "handbook" (see below) to help equip Christians for their ministry at work.

Continuation after I moved on: A new Co-ordinator has been appointed, still working in partnership with St Peter's Saltley Trust, and is taking the project forward.

Relevant publications:

The Kingdom at Work Project: A Communal Approach to Mission in the Workplace (Peterborough: Upfront Publishing, 2014).

The Kingdom at Work Project: A Handbook, pp. 24–8. Obtainable in digital form from rev.julian.e.blakemore@gmail.com.

All the *Bulletins* can be downloaded from:
<http://www.saltleytrust.org.uk/faith-and-work-in-theological-education-and-training/>, accessed 12 May 2023.

The Bakewell Asylum Seekers and Refugees Programme

Category: Individuals and groups
  The time involved: 2016–23
  My roles: strategist, intermediary, enabler and partner—To harness and co-ordinate the contributions of those in the Bakewell area concerned about the situation of asylum seekers and refugees in the UK to do everything possible to improve their lot.
  Status of the project: A voluntary ecumenical initiative.
  Location and staff: Undertaken mostly online from my home in Bakewell with myself as Co-ordinator (voluntary).
  Participants: Christians, churches, schools and others in the area. Over 100 people on the emailing list.
  Gatherings and events: Occasional day meetings. vigils, market stall, fundraising initiatives and clothing collection.
  Organization: English teaching, hospitality days for refugees from nearby cities, advocacy and fundraising groups.
  Links with the institutional church: All the local churches involved. No contacts beyond the Bakewell area.
  Methods of sustaining, developing and publicizing the movement: The network has a regular *e-Newsletter*. The groups take initiatives related to their specified functions.
  Continuation: Ongoing.

I hope the above initiatives demonstrate that the designation of deacon as a servant leader within the diaconal church as movement has a role that is both important and feasible, and which can further the process of communal transformation of church, society and world.

Nevertheless, the inability of the institutional church of today to recognize the significance of such initiatives, and the importance of the diaconal leadership roles needed to facilitate them, reveals just how hard it is for a presbyteral hierarchy to understand what it means to be a diaconal church. Such a lack of awareness arises from that church's inability to grasp that a theology of the kingdom community, and the commissioning of the laity as its instruments for communal transformation, must be at the heart of its theology and practice of mission. Until the church of today can cease promoting itself as "a church-centred kingdom" and become a kingdom-centred, and thus diaconal, church in the form of both collective *and* movement, it will be unable to engage effectively with "a new era" in which it is crucial that humankind comes together to tackle the potentially terminal crises humankind now faces.

Bibliography

Almeida, P., *Social Movements: The Structure of Collective Mobilization* (Oakland, CA: University of California Press, 2019).

Arias, M., *Announcing the Reign of God: Evangelization and the Subversive Memory of Jesus* (Philadelphia: Fortress Press, 1984).

Avis, P., *Reconciling Theology: Conflict and Convergence in Theology and Church* (London: SCM Press, 2022).

Bauman, Z., *Community: Seeking Safety in an Insecure World* (Cambridge: Polity Press, 2001).

Berger, P. and Luckmann, T., *The Social Construction of Reality* (Harmondsworth: Penguin, 1966, 1984).

Blackshaw, T., *Key Concepts in Community Studies* (London: Sage, 2010).

Brown, K., *Xi: A Study in Power* (London: Icon Books, 2022).

Brown, R., "The Deacon in Worship: A Ministry of Hospitality", in *The Diaconate in Ecumenical Perspective: Ecclesiology, Liturgy and Practice* (Durham: Sacristy Press, 2019), pp. 161–7.

Called to Love and Praise: A Methodist Conference Statement on the Church (1999) (Peterborough: Methodist Publishing House, 1999).

Called to Transformation—Ecumenical Diakonia (Geneva: World Council of Churches, 2022).

CIPL—Christians in Public Life Programme (various dates) (Birmingham: Westhill College [A selection of these papers is published in D. Clark (1997), *Changing World, Unchanging Church?*])

Clark, D., *Community and a Suburban Village* (Unpublished PhD thesis, University of Sheffield, 1969).

Clark, D., "The Concept of Community—a Re-examination", *The Sociological Review* 21:3 (1973).

Clark, D., "The Church as Symbolic Place", *Epworth Review* 2:1 (1974).

Clark, D., *Basic Christian Communities: Towards an Alternative Society* (London: SPCK, 1977).

Clark, D., *The Liberation of the Church: The Role of Basic Christian Groups in a New Re-formation* (Birmingham, Westhill College: The National Centre for Christian Communities and Networks, 1984).

Clark, D., *Yes to Life: In Search of the Kingdom Community* (London: Collins, 1987).

Clark, D., *Community Education: Towards a Framework for the Future* (Birmingham: Westhill College, 1989).

Clark, D., *Schools as Learning Communities: Transforming Education* (London: Cassell, 1996).

Clark, D., *Changing World, Unchanging Church?* (London: Mowbray, 1997).

Clark, D., *Breaking the Mould of Christendom: Kingdom Community, Diaconal Church and the Liberation of the Laity* (Peterborough: Epworth Press, 2005).

Clark, D. (ed.), *The Diaconal Church: Beyond the Mould of Christendom* (Peterborough: Epworth Press, 2008).

Clark, D. (ed.), *Reshaping the Mission of Methodism* (Oldham: Church in the Market Place, 2010), pp. 167–91.

Clark, D., *Building the Human City: The Origins and Future Potential of the Human City Institute (1995–2002)* (2011). Available at <https://humancityinstitute.wordpress.com/reports/>, accessed 9 May 2023.

Clark, D., *The Kingdom at Work Project: A Communal Approach to Mission in the Workplace* (Peterborough: Upfront Publishing, 2014).

Clark, D., *Building Kingdom Communities: With the Diaconate as a New Order of Mission* (Peterborough: Upfront Publishing, 2016).

Clark, D., *The Gift of a Renewed Diaconate—and the Contribution of British Methodism* (Peterborough: FastPrint Publishing, 2018).

Clark, D. and Staton, M., "Towards a renewed diaconate: Signposts from *The Diaconate in Ecumenical Perspective*" (2019), available at <https://sites.google.com/view/skdiaconate2018/articles>, accessed 12 May 2023.

Clements, K. W., *J. H. Oldham and George Bell: Ecumenical Pioneers* (Minneapolis, MN: Fortress Press, 2022).
Cohen, A. P., *The Symbolic Construction of Community* (London: Ellis Harwood and Tavistock, 1985).
Colley, L., *The Gun, the Ship and the Pen: Warfare, Constitutions, and the Making of the Modern World* (London: Profile Books, 2021).
Collins, J. N., *Diakonia: Re-interpreting the Ancient Sources* (New York: Oxford University Press, 1990).
Collins, J. N., *Diakonia Studies: Critical Issues in Ministry* (New York: Oxford University Press, 2014).
The Common Good and the Catholic Church's Social Teaching: A statement by the Catholic Bishops' Conference of England and Wales (London: The Catholic Church's Bishops' Conference of England and Wales, 1996).
Compendium of the Social Doctrine of the Roman Catholic Church (English edition) (London: Continuum, 2005).
Cone, James H., *A Black Theology of Liberation* (Philadelphia, PA: Lippincott, 1970).
Congar, Y. M. J., *Lay People in the Church: A Study for the Theology of the Laity*, tr. D. Attwater (Westminster, MD: Newman Press, 1957).
della Porta, D. and Diani, M., *Social Movements: An Introduction*, 3rd edn (Oxford: Wiley Blackwell, 2022).
Devetak, R. et al. (eds), *Theories of International Relations*, 6th edn (London: Bloomsbury Academic, 2022).
Dodd, C. H., *The Parables of the Kingdom*, revised edn (London: Collins Fount, 1961).
Dollard, K., Marett-Crosby, A. and (Abbot) Wright, T., *Doing Business with Benedict: The Rule of Saint Benedict and Business Management: A Conversation* (London: Continuum, 2002).
Duffy, Eamon, *The Stripping of the Altars*, 2nd edn (London: Yale University Press, 2005).
Dulles, A., *Models of the Church* (London: Gill & Macmillan, 1974, expanded edn 2002).
The Forgotten Trinity: The BCC Study Commission on Trinitarian Doctrine Today (London: Churches Together in Britain and Ireland, 2011).

Francis (Pope), *Laudato Si': On care for our common home* (London: Catholic Truth Society, 2015).

Francis (Pope), *Fratelli Tutti: On fraternity and social friendship* (Huntington, IN: OSV, 2020).

Fukuyama, F., *The End of History and the Last Man* (London: Penguin, 1992).

Galeotti, M., *A Short History of Russia: From the Pagans to Putin* (London: Ebury Press, 2021).

Gibbs, M. and Morton, T. R., *God's Frozen People* (London: Fontana/Collins, 1964).

Gibbs, M. and Morton, T. R., *God's Lively People* (London: Fontana/Collins, 1971).

Gilbert, A. D., *Religion and Society in Industrial England: Church, Chapel, and Social Change, 1740–1914* (London: Longman, 1976).

Gooder, Paula, "'Diakonia' in the New Testament—a dialogue with John N. Collins", *Ecclesiology* 3:1 (2006), pp. 33–56.

Gooder, P., "Towards a diaconal church: Some reflections on New Testament material", in D. Clark (ed.), *The Diaconal Church: Beyond the Mould of Christendom* (Peterborough: Epworth Press, 2008), pp. 99–108.

Gore, A., *The Future* (London: W. H. Allen, 2013).

Graeber, D. and Wengrow, D., *The Dawn of Everything: A New History of Humanity* (London: Allen Lane, 2021).

Greenleaf, R. K., *Servant Leadership* (Valdosta, GA: Greenleaf Centre, 2012 [1970]).

Hawtin, D. and Paul, R., *The Origin and Development of Local Ecumenical Partnerships: Telling the Story* (2011, re-issued 2020) at <https://cte.org.uk/working-together/local/local-ecumenical-partnerships-leps/lep-literature/telling-the-story-the-origin-and-development-of-leps/>, accessed 9 May 2023.

Hillery, G. A., "Definitions of Community: Areas of Agreement", *Rural Sociology* 20:2 (1955), pp. 111–23.

Holland, T., *Dominion: The Making of the Western Mind* (London: Abacus, 2019).

Horrell, David, *Solidarity and Difference: A Contemporary Reading of Paul's Ethics* (London: Bloomsbury T&T Clark, 2016).

Hughes, J., *The End of Work: Theological Critiques of Capitalism* (Oxford: Blackwell Publishing, 2007).
Hull, J. M., *School Worship: An Obituary* (London: SCM Press, 1975).
Hull, J. M., *What Prevents Christian Adults from Learning?* (London: SCM Press, 1985).
Jackson, D. M. (ed.), *The Diaconate in Ecumenical Perspective: Ecclesiology, Liturgy and Practice* (Durham: Sacristy Press, 2019).
Jackson, D. M., "The Diaconate in the Anglican and Luther Traditions: an Anglican Perspective", *Consensus* 43:1 (2022).
Jenkins, D., *The Glory of Man* (London: SCM Press, 1966).
Jenkins, D., *The Contradiction of Christianity* (London: SCM Press, 1976).
Jones, Gloria Maria, "Women and the Diaconate: A Roman Catholic Perspective", in D. M. Jackson (ed.), *The Diaconate in Ecumenical Perspective: Ecclesiology, Liturgy and Practice* (Durham: Sacristy Press, 2019), pp. 72–8.
Katz, R. et al. (eds), *Gen Z Explained: The Art of Living in a Digital Age* (Chicago: University of Chicago Press, 2021).
Khanna, P., *Move: How Mass Migration Will Reshape the World* (London: Weidenfeld & Nicolson, 2022).
Kraemer, H., *A Theology of the Laity* (Philadelphia, PA: Westminster Press, 1958).
Larive, A. L., *After Sunday: A Theology of Work* (New York: Continuum, 2004).
Lewis, C. S., *The Four Loves* (London: Fontana Books, 1963).
MacCulloch, D., *A History of Christianity* (London: Allen Lane, 2009).
MacIntyre, A., *After Virtue: A Study in Moral Theory*, 2nd edn (London: Duckworth, 1985).
MacIver, R. M. and Page, C. H., *Society: An Introductory Analysis* (London: Macmillan, 1950).
MacMillan, M., *The War that Ended Peace: How Europe Abandoned Peace for the First World War* (London: Profile Books, 2013).
Marsh, C., *The Beloved Community: How Faith Shapes Social Justice from the Civil Rights Movement to Today* (New York: Basic Books (Perseus), 2005).

Marshall, T., *Divided: Why We're Living in an Age of Walls* (London: Elliott & Thompson Limited, 2018).

Maslow, A. H., "A theory of human motivation", *Psychological Review* 50:4 (1943), pp. 370–96.

McLeod, H. and Ustorf, W. (eds), *The Decline of Christendom in Western Europe, 1750–2000* (Cambridge: Cambridge University Press, 2003).

Moltmann, J., *The Crucified God: The Cross of Christ as the Foundation and Criticism of Christian Theology*, tr. R. A. Wilson and J. Bowden (London: SCM Press, 1973).

Moltmann, J., *The Trinity and Kingdom of God*, tr. Margaret Kohl (London: SCM Press, 1981).

Moltmann, J., *God for a Secular Society*, tr. Margaret Kohl (London: SCM Press, 1999).

Newbigin, L., *Your Kingdom Come* (Leeds: John Paul, The Preacher's Press, 1980).

Nisbet, R. A., *The Quest for Community* (Wilmington, DE: ISI Books, 2010 [1953]).

Otto, R., *The Idea of the Holy* (Oxford: Oxford University Press, 1968 [1923]).

Parry (Abbot) (tr.) and de Waal, E., *The Rule of Saint Benedict* (Leominster: Gracewing, 1995).

Peden, A., "Integrity of Vocation and the Transitional Diaconate", in D. M. Jackson (ed.), *The Diaconate in Ecumenical Perspective: Ecclesiology, Liturgy and Practice* (Durham: Sacristy Press, 2019), pp. 43–52.

Plant, R., *Community and Ideology: An Essay in Applied Social Philosophy* (London: Routledge & Kegan Paul, 1974).

Poole, E., *Capitalism's Toxic Assumptions: Redefining Next Generation Economics* (London: Bloomsbury, 2015).

Quaker Faith and Practice (QFP), 3rd edn (London: Religious Society of Friends, 2005).

Robinson, J. A. T., "The meaning of the Eucharist", in *Where Three Ways Meet* (London: SCM Press, 1977).

Rowlands, Anna, *Towards a Politics of Communion: Catholic Social Teaching in Dark Times* (London: T&T Clark, 2021).

Ryan, B., *How the West Was Lost: The Decline of a Myth and the Search for New Stories* (London: Hurst & Company, 2019).

Sandel, M., *What Money Can't Buy: The Moral Limits of Markets* (New York: Farrar, Straus and Giroux, 2012).

Sandercock, L., *Towards Cosmopolis: Planning for Multicultural Cities* (Chichester: John Wiley & Sons, 1998).

Saul, J. R., *The Collapse of Globalism* (London: Atlantic Books, 2018).

Schumacher, E. F., *Small Is Beautiful: A Study of Economics as if People Mattered* (London: Blond & Briggs, 1973).

Senge, P. M., *The Fifth Discipline: The Art and Practice of the Learning Organization* (New York: Currency Doubleday, 1990).

Setting God's People Free (London: Archbishops' Council, 2017).

Siedentop, L., *Inventing the Individual: The Origins of Western Liberalism* (London: Allen Lane, 2014).

Simpson, G., *Conflict and Community: A Study in Social Theory* (New York: Liberal Press, 1937).

Snyder, H. A., *Models of the Kingdom* (Eugene, OR: Wipf & Stock, 2001, previously published by Abingdon Press, 1991).

The Spiritual Exercises of Saint Ignatius Loyola, ed. and tr. G. Hughes and M. Ivens (Leominster: Gracewing, 2004).

Tawney, R. H., *Religion and the Rise of Capitalism* (West Drayton: Pelican, 1948 [1926]).

Thangaraj, M. T., *The Common Task: A Theology of Christian Mission* (Nashville, TN: Abingdon Press, 1999).

Tomlin, G., *Bound to be Free: The Paradox of Freedom* (London: Bloomsbury, 2017).

Tönnies, F., *Community and Society*, tr. C. P. Loomis (London: Routledge and Kegan Paul, 1955 [1887]).

Turner, J., "Islam as a theory of international relations?" (2009) at <https://www.e-ir.info/2009/08/03/islam-as-a-theory-of-international-relations/>, accessed 5 May 2023.

Vioti, P., "Nationalism vs. Internationalism: Fears, Uncertainties and Geopolitics in Europe", in R. Belloni et al. (eds), *Fear and Uncertainty in Europe: The Return to Realism?* (Cham: Palgrave Macmillan, 2019), pp. 35–52.

Volf, M., *Work in the Spirit: Toward a Theology of Work* (Eugene, OR: Wipf & Stock, 1991).
Volf, M., *Exclusion and Embrace: A Theological Exploration of Identity, Otherness and Reconciliation* (Nashville, TN: Abingdon Press, 2019).
de Waal, E., *The Celtic Way of Prayer* (London: Hodder & Stoughton, 1996).
Weber, M., *The Protestant Ethic and the Spirit of Capitalism* (Oxford: Oxford University Press, 2010 [1905]).
Wenger, E., *Communities of Practice: Learning, Meaning and Identity* (Cambridge: Cambridge University Press, 1998).
Wenger, E., McDermott, R. and Snyder, W. M., *Cultivating Communities of Practice: A Guide to Managing Knowledge* (Boston, MA: Harvard Business School Press, 2002).
What is a Deacon? Methodist Conference Report, 2004.
Williams, A., *The Christian Left* (Cambridge: Polity Press, 2022).
Williams, C., *John Wesley's Theology Today* (London: Epworth Press, 1960).
Williams, R., *The Way of St Benedict* (London: Bloomsbury, 2020).

EU GPSR Authorized Representative:

LOGOS EUROPE, 9 rue Nicolas Poussin, 17000 La Rochelle, France

contact@logoseurope.eu